MANAGEMENT AT A GLANCE

MANAGEMENT AT A GLANCE

FOR
TOP, MIDDLE AND LOWER EXECUTIVES

Ahmed Shehu Awak, PhD

authorHOUSE®

AuthorHouse™
1663 Liberty Drive
Bloomington, IN 47403
www.authorhouse.com
Phone: 1-800-839-8640

© 2012 by Ahmed Shehu Awak, PhD. All rights reserved.

No part of this book may be reproduced, stored in a retrieval system, or transmitted by any means without the written permission of the author.

Published by AuthorHouse   10/08/2012

ISBN: 978-1-4772-3777-9 (sc)
ISBN: 978-1-4772-3778-6 (e)

Any people depicted in stock imagery provided by Thinkstock are models, and such images are being used for illustrative purposes only.
Certain stock imagery © Thinkstock.

This book is printed on acid-free paper.

Because of the dynamic nature of the Internet, any web addresses or links contained in this book may have changed since publication and may no longer be valid. The views expressed in this work are solely those of the author and do not necessarily reflect the views of the publisher, and the publisher hereby disclaims any responsibility for them.

Dedication

This book is dedicated to humanity for the sake of knowledge.

Preface

This book is intended to provide a summarized knowledge of the various fields that make up the management discipline, for executives and other intending and potential entrepreneurs and managers to keep abreast of the various activities in several departments of their organizations, which they are responsible for eventual outcomes, in one way or another.

The desire for this book was borne out of the fact that executives and other managers and entrepreneurs: Doctors, Engineers, Lawyers, Proprietors, Government officials etc may find it convenient as a handbook to acquire the introductory knowledge of management and administration in order to enhance their conceptual skills.

The book is built on both theoretical and practical information, brief and concise, geared towards driving home points and tips for useful conceptualization. It has been fashioned in an easy to read and understand and format.

All over the world, a lot of emphasis is laid on effective governance, both in public and private sectors of the economy, so as to have improved systems and standards of living. It is hoped that a hand book of this sort will come in handy. Great effort has been made to avoid making the textbook voluminous. It has been divided into topics according to various fields to provide easier access of the contents.

Acknowledgement

"No man is an island", they say. I am grateful to all friends and colleagues that contributed in one way or the other towards this book. Dangana, PhD, thanks a lot. Mrs. Ochiagha, Uchenna Thessy, who typed and retyped times without number, thanks a lot too, Dr. Bashir(bobo),thanks and don't forget project two. My family, nuclear and extended thanks for the love and support. My Author house family, thanks for a beautiful job.

Contents

TOPIC ONE: Management Theory

Evolution of Management 1
Pre-Colonial Theory 2
The Scientific Management Theory 2
Administrative Theory: 3
The Behaviorist/Human Relation
    Management Theory 5
Organizational Theory 6
Operation Research Theory: 6
The System Theory: 6
Contingency Theory: 6
Definition of Management 7
Management Functions: 8
Who is a Manager? 13
Managerial Roles 13
Tasks of Managers 15

TOPIC TWO: Human Resources Management

The Domain of Managing Human Resources 22
Human Resource Management Activities 24
Human Resoruce Skills For Managers 25
Functions of Management 26
The Role of conceptual, technical and
    human skills 27
Compensation: Theory And Administration 29
Benefits 31
Human Resource Planning 32
Personnel Staffing And Evaluation 32
Performance Evaluation: 33
Job Analysis 33
Recruitment and selection 34

TOPIC THREE: Marketing Management

Company orientations towards the market place 37
The production concept 37
The product concept 37
The societal marketing concept 38
The selling concept 38
The marketing concept 38
Marketing Channels 38
Work performed by marketing channels: 40
Channel functions 40
Channel levels: 41
Service Sector channel 41
Channel Decisions 41
Factors determining channel decisions 42
Logistics Strategy 42
Nature and importance of physical
    distribution and marketing logistics: 43
Major logistics functions 44
Designing International Distribution Channels: 45
Integrated logistics management 45
Promotional Campaigns 46
Advertisement 47
Sales Promotion 48
Personal Selling 49
Public Relations 50
Retail Management 50
Types of Retailers 51
Retailer Marketing Decisions 52
Retail organizations 52
Target Market Decisions 53

TOPIC FOUR: Global Marketing

Understanding the global environment 56
The international trade system 56
Deciding whether to go international 57

TOPIC FIVE: Computer In Business

Computer in businesses 59
Impact of computers on organizations 61

TOPIC SIX: Cost Management Systems

Cost object: 62
Direct Cost and Indirect Cost Objects 62

TOPIC SEVEN: Entrepreneurship

Functions of the entrepreneur 65
Characteristics of an Entrepreneur 65
Salary Employment versus Entrepreneurship 66
Problems associated with salaried employment 66
Advantages and disadvantages of entrepreneurship . 66
Role of financial system 68
Financial System 68

TOPIC EIGHT: Financial Institutions, Markets And Economy

Financial Intermediation 69
Financial markets 69
Money markets 70
Capital markets 70

TOPIC NINE: Financial Reporting

Financial management 72
Management of Cash 72
Reasons for holding cash 73

TOPIC TEN: International Real Estate

International Overview 75
Globalization of Real Estate Practice 76

TOPIC ELEVEN: Management Accounting

Introduction to Management Accounting: 77
Usage of Accounting Information 77

TOPIC TWELVE: Portfolio Management

Investment defined 79
Stock 79
Why do corporations issue stock? 80
Investment decisions 81
Raising money for investments 82
Managing Risks 82

TOPIC THIRTEEN: Labour Management Relations

Industry classifications 83
Labor 84
Management 84
Natural resources 84
Collective Bargaining 84
Types of Unions 85
Labor union 85

TOPIC FOURTEEN: Multinational Business Finance

Foreign Exchange Markets and Participants 86
The (IMF) International Monetary Fund in
    Multinational Business Finance 87
The World Bank in Multinational Business Finance 88
Central Banks in Multinational Business Finance ... 89

TOPIC FIFTEEN: Organization And Management Process

Division of Labor and Coordination 90
Coordinating work activities................................... 91
Division of Labor 91
Informal Communications 92
Formal communication: 92
Elements of Organizational Structure: 93
Coordination through standardization.................... 93

TOPIC SIXTEEN: Organizational Behaviour

Organization: 95
The need to study Organizational Behavior............ 96
The five anchors of Organizational Behavior (OB) . 97
Knowledge management 100
Intellectual capital 100
Knowledge management process 101
Knowledge acquisition 101
Knowledge sharing.. 101
Knowledge utilization... 102
Organizational memory.. 102

TOPIC SEVENTEEN: Production Planning And Control

Production 103
Production management 103
Purchasing (Procurement) 104
Material request planning..................................... 104
Just in time (JIT) systems..................................... 105
Inspection 105
Maintenance 106

TOPIC EIGHTEEN: Real Estate Law

Public ownership 107
Special forms of ownership 108
Restrictions on ownership 109
Private restrictions on ownership 110

TOPIC NINETEEN: Residential Property Development

Factors that influence real property values: 112
Single family residential districts........................... 113
Multifamily residential districts 113
Residential layout considerations: 113

TOPIC TWENTY: Risk Management

Defining objectives:... 115
Definition of Risk 115
Threats and Opportunities 116
Risk Management 117
Strategy 118
Management 118
Business Policy 118
Policy 118

TOPIC TWENTY ONE: Strategic Management

Business Functional Policies 119
Business strategy and strategic management: 119
Corporate Strategy: 120
Business and its environment 121
Business strategy... 121
Functional strategy 121
Corporate social responsibility.............................. 122

TOPIC TWENTY TWO: The Management Of Teams

Teams 123
Team effectiveness 124
Team design and features 124
Task Characteristics: 125
Team size: 125
Team composition: 126
Team diversity: 126

Topic One

MANAGEMENT THEORY

EVOLUTION OF MANAGEMENT

The emergence of management concepts, philosophies and ideas were fundamentally traced back to the existence of man. The earlier management concepts were record keeping procedures and processes developed by Sumerian Priests 500 BC. The ancient Egyptians equally used complex management techniques. The antiquated Chinese Personnel recognized the need for management functions of planning, organizing, influencing and controlling. Plato identified the principles of division of labor and specialization while Alexander the great initiated the managerial principle of decision making.

Essentially, most of the management concepts used today was derivatives of the theories propounded by F.W. Taylor, Max Weber, Henry Fayol etc. The thoughts of Management Philosophies were grouped into phases. That is, the pre-colonial, scientific management theory, administrative theory, the behaviorist/Human Relation/Psychologists theory, organization theory, System theory and contingency theory.

Below demonstrates the abridged explanation of the management school of thoughts.

Pre-Colonial Theory

As discussed above, management concepts began with the existence of Man. The needs of a man in the nuclear, extended, formal and informal settings, community and society were prioritized so as to be satisfied accordingly. Additionally, the industrialists began to convert the raw materials into goods and services towards the satisfaction of human needs during the conversion process. This required the managerial functions of planning, forecasting, organizing, directing, commanding, coordinating and controlling. Since the needs of man became so numerous, the industrialists began to introduce sophisticated management techniques and this led to the emergence of the second phase of scientific management theory.

The Scientific Management Theory

Organizational productivity, efficiency and proficiency had given birth to scientific school of thought by Fredrick Winslow Taylor (1856-1915). The founders of this school of thought were F.W. Taylor, Henry Granth and Frank as well as Lillian Gilbert. The prime proponents of scientific/traditional, Management was Fredrick W. Taylor and he based his philosophical inclination on four principles which included the following:

(i) The Scientific selection of workers and appropriate allocation of responsibilities based on specialization.
(ii) The systematic procedure of performing specific task based on empirical findings.
(iii) Manpower development
(iv) Co-operation between management and employees.

Taylor opined that the application of the above stated principles could lead to an increase in organizational productivity and effectiveness.

Other proponents of the scientific management theory were Henry L. Granth (1861-1919), who suggested that bonus should be paid as a motivational technique to a well performed staff in addition to the wages system. He equally introduced bar charts in production scheduling and control.

Frank B. and Lillian M Gilbrath (1868-1924) and (1878-1972) respectively, promoted individual workers' welfare. Their contributions were faster productivity and enhancing organizational efficiency. However, the limitations of this theory were inappropriate incorporation of workers' needs to organizational objectives and exhortative tendency on the part of management.

ADMINISTRATIVE THEORY:

This theory was propounded by Henri Fayol (1841-1952). He observed that management was a concept to be taught as a course. He critically spelt out the managerial behavior and described management as a good process of planning, forecasting, organizing, controlling, commanding and co-coordinating. He maintained that organizational objectives could be achieved on the application of management principles. He proposed fourteen (14) principles to be integrated into the organization. These are:

1. **Division of Labor:** He believed that specialization enhanced productivity.

2. **Authority:** He clearly suggested that for work to be done efficiently, Managers must give executive orders or directives.
3. **Discipline:** He maintained that for an organization to achieve its corporate goals there must be rules and regulations, policies, strategies, procedures, guidelines and protocols and any employee who disobeys the regulations set must face a penalty.
4. **Unity of Command:** He was of the opinion that since the organizational goal, mission, vision and corporate objective is one, there must be one and uniform command from one person to avoid conflict.
5. **Unity of Direction:** He stressed that organizational objectives could be achieved by one Manager. One plan should be employed he maintained.
6. **Sub-ordination of Individual Interest to the Common Interest:** The interest of the employees should be made lower than the interest of the organization.
7. **Remuneration:** The employees should be paid adequately as well as the employers.
8. **Centralization:** He viewed that for the organization to achieve its goal, decision making should be centralized.
9. **Scalar Chains:** There should be an organizational hierarchy where information, instructions, requests, views, messages and policies flow from the highest officers to the lowest officers and vice-visa.
10. **Order:** Both human and non-human resources should be in the right place at the right time in the right organization to achieve the right objectives set.
11. **Equity:** There should be fairness, justice, transparency and diplomacy in dealing with the subordinates.

12. **Stability of Tenure of Personnel:** There should be job stability, security and organizational commitment.
13. **Initiative:** The employees should be given an opportunity to carry out their creative and innovative plans.
14. **Espirit de corps:** The employees should be given the opportunity to work together as a team to achieve a common purpose.

The contributions made by Fayol were complemented by Luther Gulik and Lyndak Urwick.

The Administrative theory propounded by the above named proponents was targeted towards bringing out the functions and principles of management and the job of a manager.

THE BEHAVIORIST/HUMAN RELATION MANAGEMENT THEORY

This school of thought was pioneered by Prof. Elton Mayo and Fritz Roethlisberger. They clearly spelt out that for an organization to achieve its corporate goals, the behavior, psychology and manner of the employees had to be studied. They observed that the accomplishment of an organization's objectives of effectiveness, profitability, cost minimization and productivity could also be made if the employees were allowed to work together as a team, the formation of informal sector as well as friendship. The theory was centered on the concepts of motivation, leadership and workgroup. The Hawthorne studies were the genesis of human relations movement. Other proponents were Mary Parker Follett (1863-1933) and Munsterberg Hugo (1863-1916).

ORGANIZATIONAL THEORY

This theory was propounded by a German Sociologist called Max Weber (1864-1920). He suggested that bureaucracy was the best way of managing a big organization. Four elements of his postulation were highlighted. He discovered division of labor, hierarchy of organization, formal rules and regulations, job description and employees' recruitment and selection. He also discovered the elements of organization which included sharing of common purpose, communication and co-operation. To him, Managerial functions were to provide a system of communication, individual security and formulating organizational purpose.

OPERATION RESEARCH THEORY:

This school of thought used mathematical models like job assignment, queuing theory, linear programming, transportation model, Performance Evaluation Review Technique etc in decision making.

THE SYSTEM THEORY:

This approach saw an organization as a purposeful, result-oriented, unified, corporate and integrated system made up of interrelated parts. That an organization was made up of open and close systems. This approach was identified by Blending (1956).

CONTINGENCY THEORY:

This theory is also known as situational theory developed and applied by managers, consultants and researchers who desired to apply the concepts of management into real life situations. They were of the view that a supportive plan or derivative plan should be made if the main plan fails in the process of its implementation.

DEFINITION OF MANAGEMENT

Parker (1964) defined management as "an art of getting things done through other people". The economists analyzed that the **"Things to be done"** are termed as Input variables of Land, Labor, capital and entrepreneurship. The harmonization and effective integration of the factors of production during Manufacturing to produce goods and services for the satisfaction of human needs is termed management. The output variables of goods and services are classified as the **"Done things"**. Basically, Management is defined as the operational process of planning, organizing, motivating and controlling of both human and non-human resources to achieve organizational objectives of profit maximization, cost minimization, share-holder maximization, survival, growth, sales maximization, stability and market share leadership. It is the allocation and appropriate administration of resources to achieve departmental goals and organizational overall corporate objectives.

Wren (1979) defined management as an activity essential to organize endeavors to perform certain functions of obtaining the effective acquisition, allocation and utilization of human efforts and physical resources for the purpose of accomplishing some goals. Burton and Taker (1997) added that management is the process of planning, organizing, heading and controlling the resources of an organization in the efficient and effective pursuit of specified organizational goals.

Fayol (1916) defined management as the social process of planning, organizing, commanding, controlling and motivating resources to achieve organizational objectives. Breach (1976) maintained that management is an operational process of planning, forecasting, organizing, co-coordinating and directing resources to achieve objectives. Mintzgberg (1984) said that management is known by the roles he performs in the course of performing his obligations. The role of the manager is classified into three, he said these are:

1. **Interpersonal Role:** That a manager is a figure head, liaison, leader etc.
2. **Informational Role:** That a manager is a monitor and disseminator.
3. **Decisional Role:** That a manager is a negotiator, disturbance handler, decision maker etc.

Management Functions:

Heterogamous Management experts agreed on four acceptable management functions which is acronym "POMC". These are Planning, Organizing, Motivating and Controlling. These functions shall be treated accordingly thus:

Planning:

Planning is defined as the determination, formation, allocation, administration and effective utilization of the alternative courses of action to achieve organizational objectives. It is grouped into three ramifications: Short term planning, medium term planning and long term planning.

Short Term Planning

This is also known as operational planning. It is the determination and allocation of resources to be achieved within a year.

Medium Term Planning

The realization of organizational objectives is within the span of four years. It is also known as tactical planning.

Long Term Planning

This is otherwise known as corporate planning or strategic planning. It is the commitment of resources into action for the purpose of achieving organizational efficiency and effectiveness within the period of five years and above.

Process of Planning

In achieving the organizational objectives, a process must be followed religiously. The planning process includes defining the objectives, analyzing the environment, determining the alternative courses of action, evaluating the courses of action, selecting a course of action, formulating supporting plan, budgeting the plan and implementing the plan.

Planning is said to be the bedrock of organizational success. It is therefore the process of establishing the main direction and organizational objectives and selecting future course of action to achieve expected result.

Organizing:

The second managerial function is technically referred to as organizing. Once planning is established, business structure has to be designed, hierarchy has to be set, job responsibilities, job description, job enlargement, job enrichment, job title and job specification have to be formulated by the Managing Directors, Chief Executive Officers, Consultants, Management Experts, Technical Working Groups etc. to achieve organizational objectives. Organizing could be by departmentalization, Territorial, Product and Authority.

It is a managerial function of determining all activities necessary to achieve the set plans, grouping such activities, assigning the activities by positions and delegating managerial authority.

Motivating:

This is the third managerial function. It is the process of stimulating the needs, motives, desires, drives and intentions of the employees to achieve organizational objectives. Schein (1964) opined that there are four levels of motivation in an employee. These are:

1. An employer is a Social Economic Man (SEM). That is, he needs to be rewarded, compensated and retained in his working place. Whatever thing he does, he needs gain and profit.
2. An employee is a Self-Actualizing Man (SAM). He maintained that man needs self-esteem, self-recognition and self fulfillment in the process of performing his civic responsibilities.

3. An employee is a rational man: This explains that man also wants to be an achiever by all means.
4. An employee is a complex man. He observed that whatever one does, no one can satisfy man because of the nature of radicalism and sophisticated behavior.

For the purpose of understanding the concept of motivation, two approaches have been used termed "CAPA" approach. "CA" means Content Approach and "PA" Process Approach.

Content Approach (CA)

This approach spells out the basic and fundamental things that motivate a Man. Many Scholars (Traditional) discussed comprehensively about the content approach. They include Abraham Maslow's Hierarchy of needs. He grouped the needs of man to be satisfied hierarchically. These are the physiological needs, security needs, social needs, esteem needs and self-actualization needs. McGregor theory of X and Y, Douglas theory of hygiene factors, needs-achievement theory, maturity and immaturity theory of Victor Vroom etc. These specify that the needs, aspirations, expectations and motives of an employee must be satisfied.

Process Approach (PA)

This approach dictates the reasons for motivation. Modern theories were vividly discussed. The theories include Expectancy theory, Equity theory, Re-enforcement theory etc.

Controlling

This is the process of achieving organizational objectives by establishing standards, comparing measured performance against established standards and reinforcing successes as well as correcting deviations. It is classified into directing, coordinating, communicating and decision making.

Directing

This is a subset of controlling. It is an executive order to achieve organizational goals. It is the process where policies, orders, instructions, messages, reports, issues, strategies, procedures, protocols, rules and regulations as well as feedback mechanisms are being channeled.

Coordinating

This is the integration and harmonization of both human and non-human resources to achieve results.

Communicating

This is the process of passing or transmitting messages, information, ideas, instructions, policies, strategies and feedback from one person to another. The process of communication includes the sender, the message, receiver, channel and feedback. The main forms of communication are written and oral communication.

Decision Making

Managerial decision making is the practical and proactive approach to solve the identified problems in the process of achieving the corporate objectives of the organization.

WHO IS A MANAGER?

A Manager is a trained and well experienced professional who assumes organization position in achieving the goals of an enterprise. He is a person who influences the efforts of others and harnesses both human and non-material resources to achieve the organizational goals. He is a person who uses and applies the four Managerial functions discussed above to achieve results.

MANAGERIAL ROLES

A role is something wider than a mere job description with emphasis on duties and activities. A role also includes the behavior that is expected of a person in fulfilling a job.

Apart from the interrelated activities which all managers must undertake as a process (Planning, organizing, leading and controlling); there are specific roles that managers may fill at various times.

There have been many studies of the top managers' job. Henry Mintzberg in his book, "The Nature of Managerial Work"' described the manager's work as consisting of ten different but highly interrelated roles. These roles are separated into three basic groupings; Interpersonal roles, informational roles and decisional roles. The Interpersonal roles arise from a manager's formal authority and put the manager in a position to fulfill the informational roles, which is derived from the information gathering accomplished by the manager as a liaison. Interpersonal and informational roles support the decisional roles, which require managers to use information as an input to decision making. These roles can be used to describe any manager's job.

Interpersonal Roles

These roles derive from the formal authority and status of top management. The interpersonal roles of a manager include:

a. Figure head—Serving as enterprise representative in all social and legal matters. Thus they perform ceremonial duties or "make appearances".
b. Leader—Influencing the activities of subordinates thus inspiring them to fulfill the unit's purpose. This also involves hiring, training and motivating employees.
c. Liaison—Interacting with people outside the vertical chain of command to gain knowledge.

Informational Roles

These roles consist of the many interactions that top management engages in that involve the exchange of knowledge. These roles are:-

a. Monitor—Gathering information from a network of contacts that enable them to deal more effectively with events within an enterprise, as well as with developments in the external environment.

b. Disseminators—Sharing and distributing information internally to peers, subordinates and superiors who need it.
c. Spokesman—Transmitting information externally to customers, suppliers, business partners (peers), etc.

Decisional Roles

The following decisional roles can be identified:

a. Entrepreneur—Looking out for new ideas to bring about changes that can improve the enterprise performance. They must also be willing to adapt to changing conditions.
b. Disturbance Handler—Responding to all unforeseen pressures, crises and problems.
c. Resource Allocator—Resources include people, money, materials and information. The manager decides who will get what resources, as well as clarifies who can make what decision about which resources.
d. Negotiator—Bargain with various individuals or representatives or other enterprises, sometimes acting as intermediary and sometimes on his or her own behalf.

TASKS OF MANAGERS

A manager has two specific tasks. The first is creation of a true whole that is larger than the sum of its parts, a productive entity that turns out more than the sum of the resources put into it. This task requires the manager to make effective, whatever strength there is in his resources, and neutralize whatever there is of weakness. It also requires the manager to balance and harmonize major functions of the organization that is, managing the business, managing workers and work, and managing the enterprise in community and society. This task also requires that the manager in every one of his acts consider simultaneously the performance and results of the enterprise as a whole and the diverse activities needed to achieve synchronized performance.

The second task of the manager is to harmonize in every decision and action the requirements of immediate and long range future. He must calculate the sacrifices he makes today for the sake of tomorrow.

He must limit either sacrifice as much as possible and he must correct the damage it inflicts as soon as possible.

Management Level

Managers can/and do practice at different levels in an organization with different ranges of organizational activities. While all managers perform the same functions, there are yet differences among their jobs.

In most enterprises, there are three distinct but over-lapping levels of management. It is pertinent to understand how managerial activities at different levels relate to one another.

First-Line/Lower Manager

This is management's first line of contact with labor. They directly manage non managerial employees and do not supervise other managers. It is the first line manager's job to ensure that the plans developed by upper levels management are fulfilled by the employees who actually produce the goods and supply services. Examples of first line managers are the foreman or productive supervisor in a manufacturing plant, the technical supervisor in a research department, and the clerical supervisor in a large office. First level managers are often referred to as "Supervisors".

Middle Managers

They occupy roles positioned above first line management and below top management. The term middle management can include more than one level in an organization. Middle manager's principal responsibilities are to direct the activities that implement their organization's policies and to balance the demands of their managers with the capabilities of their employees. Middle managers thus manage other managers and serve as a link between top management and the first line management (They are integrators). They direct the activities of lower level managers and sometimes those of operating employees as well. Middle management is often seen as the prime training ground for future top level managers. They are the departmental managers, functional managers (personnel manager, accountant) etc.

Top Managers

These are responsible for the overall management of an organization. They shape enterprises objectives and do what is necessary on the highest levels. They are called executives (Chief) presidents or chairpersons of the board. They establish operating policies and guide the organization's interactions with its environment.

Functional Areas of Management

The realization of organizational objectives is essentially based on the adequate management of the functional areas of management. These are: Human Resources Management, Production Management, Financial Management, Marketing Management, Management Information System, Research and Development Management etc. These functional areas are integrated together to achieve a common organizational purpose. They will be treated one after the other.

Human Resource Management (HRM)

From the definition of Management by Parker (1964) that Management is an art of getting things done through people, the harmonization and harnessing of human and non-human resources to achieve organizational defined goals can only be made possible through people—people here refer to men. Etymologically, Human resource management was called Labor Management, People management, men management, personnel management and in the 21st century, it is called Human Resource Management.

It is essential to note that Material cannot dream. Money cannot dream and machine cannot dream. The only resource that can dream, conceptualize ideas, design structure, formulate policy and strategy, implement ideas and plans towards the actualization of an organizational goal is human resource. Human Resource has nine Cs that makes him visualize success, expand carefully and set the organizational vision, mission and guiding principles. The nine "Cs" that makes him different from other resources are commitment, competence, congruence, cost-effectives, confidence, curiosity, courageousness, constancy and character. The nine "I"s that distinguishes human resource from other resources is instinct, intuition, instrumentality, idea, initiative, industry, institution, inertia and intelligence. These implicit qualities make him unique in planning, organizing, motivating and controlling to achieve expected outcomes.

Human Resource brings the organization into existence. Management is the process of planning, organizing, motivating and controlling the material and human resources to achieve organizational objectives. Therefore, in marrying the two terms together, Human Resource Management is defined as the process of planning, organizing, motivating and controlling both human and non-human resources to achieve the corporate objectives of the organization. It is the art of recruitment, selection, induction, training and development, promotion, demotion, transfer, retrenchment, dismissal and reward of an employee to achieve an organizational objective. Human Resource Management has five main activities. These are Staffing, employee Maintenance, employee development, employee relations and reward. The efficient and effective management of human resource brings about the realization of organizational objectives.

Production Management

This deals with the conversion of input factors of production which consist of land, labor, capital and entrepreneurship into output of goods and services. Production is said to be completed when the goods produced reaches the final consumers. As a manager, you are expected to plan for the right raw materials, establishment of warehouse, and qualitative product, and control standard, supply of machinery and right channels of production.

Financial Management

This is the effective and efficient acquisition, administration, disbursement and appropriate utilization of funds to achieve organizational objectives. Financial Management specifies three major components, which are; Fund acquisition, Investment appraisal and dividend policy management. As a manager, you are required to know the various sources of funds available to your organization, working capital management, liquidity management, portfolio management, credit analysis, investment analysis and the appropriate administration of dividend.

Marketing Management

This deals with the process of designing, identifying, anticipating and satisfying the customers for a profit. It is a business activity that is designed to produce, price, promote, and distribute the goods and services to satisfy the needs of the customers with the aim of making a profit.

In marketing management, a manager is required to plan, organize and control the marketing mix of product, price, place, promotion, people, package, procedure, process and prayer very effectively. The marketing programs and organizations have to be monitored and controlled. The promotion mix of advertising, sales promotion, personal selling and publicity has to be properly utilized profitably. The market, marketing, exchange process, marketing segmentation, marketing research and intelligence, pricing strategy and international marketing have to be thoroughly planned, organized and controlled for the purpose of achieving organizational objectives.

Management Information System

Computerization and internet topologies have made the world a global village. We are flowing in the world of information. Information is defined as the assembly of data for decision making. It is the transformation of raw data. Appropriate information has to be kept for decision making.

Research and Development Management

An original, creative, innovative, synthetic and extensive product could only be gotten by research and development. This department has to be created to define business problems, proffer solutions to it and produce qualitative products that will be beneficial to the community.

Topic Two

HUMAN RESOURCES MANAGEMENT

As the CEO of your firm, do you simply dream of achieving a world standard service or product by simply employing anyone interested in working for you and letting the person do what he feels, when he feels in order to achieve your set goals and objectives? It has to be a lot more than that if you are to succeed I believe. The concept of the management of human resource is the theory of managing people at workplaces.

Business executives, practitioners and academics argued that the traditional approaches to managing workers are inappropriate and can no longer deliver the goods. To tap the full potential of workers and to provide behavior and attitudes considered necessary for competitive advantage requires three aspects of managerial control to change, which are:

(a) Organizational and job design
(b) Organizational culture
(c) Personnel policies and techniques

THE DOMAIN OF MANAGING HUMAN RESOURCES

The field of human resource management is the part of the management process that specializes in the management of people in work organizations. HRM emphasizes that employees are critical to achieving success. Sustainable competitive advantage, that human resource practices need to be integrated with corporate strategy, and that human resource specialists help organizational controllers to meet both efficiency and equity objectives.

Our broad definition of "Human Resource" would be incomplete without further explaining what we mean by such terms as 'human resources' and range of abilities, talents and attitudes, influence, productivity, quality and profitability. People set overall strategies and goals, design work systems, produce goods and services, monitor quality, allocate financial resources and market the products and services.

Individuals therefore become 'human resources' by virtue of the roles they assume in the work organizations. Employment roles are defined in a manner designed to maximize particular employee conditions to achieving organizational objectives.

In theory, the management of people is no different from the management of other resources in organizations. In practice, what makes it different is the nature of the resource people.

Organizational behavior theorists suggest that the behavior and performance of the human resource is a function of at least four variables:—ability, motivation, role, perception and situational contingencies.

The human resource differs from other resources the employer uses, partly because individuals are endowed with varying levels of ability, personality traits, gender, role, perception and differences, and partly as a result of differences in motivation and commitment. In other words, employees differ from other resources because of their ability to evaluate and to question management's actions, and their commitment and cooperation always has to be won. They have the capacity to form groups and trade unions to defend or further their economic interests.

The term "management" may be applied to either a social group or process. Classical management theorists set out to develop a science of management in which management is defined in terms of planning, organizing, commanding, coordinating and controlling.

Management is especially seen as an art. This implies that managerial activity and success depends upon traits such as intelligence, charismatic decisions, enthusiasm, integrity, dominance and self-confidence.

Human Resource Management Activities

Human resource management is a body of knowledge and a set of practices that define the nature of work and regulate the employment relationship. HRM covers the following five functional areas:

(1) **Staffing:** The obtaining of people with appropriate skills, abilities, knowledge and experience to fill jobs in the organization. Pertinent practices are human resource planning, job analysis, recruitment and selection.
(2) **Rewards:** The design and administration of reward systems. Practices include job evaluation, performance appraisal and benefits.
(3) **Employee development:** Analyzing training requirements to ensure that employees advance in the organization. Performance appraisal can identify employee key skills and "competencies".

(4) **Employee maintenance:** the administration and monitoring of workplace safety, health and welfare policies to retain a competent workforce and comply with statutory standards and regulations.

(5) **Employee Relations:** employee involvement participation schemes in union or non-union workplaces. In union environment, it also includes negotiations between management and union representatives over decisions affecting the employment contract.

HUMAN RESORUCE SKILLS FOR MANAGERS

As a manager, so many roles are played depending on the circumstance and suitability.

Managerial roles could be as a disseminator, disturbance handler, entrepreneur, figurehead, leader, liaison, monitor, negotiator, resource allocator, and spokesperson.

These roles are grouped into three categories: interpersonal, decisional and informational.

Interpersonal roles: Focuses on specific interactions with others.

> Managers often act as figure heads in managing human resources. The manager who is the head of a unit, team or department represents the people within that unit.

> For example he/she may make a presentation to the top management asking for more funds for the team's work or more time.

Leadership roles may be filled formally or informally. A manager may be assigned the formal role of a leader of a unit; other employees may emerge as leaders depending on the focus of the unit.

Decisional roles:

Each member of the organization needs to begin to think as an entrepreneur of seeking out opportunities for the firm (markets) or new ways of conducting business.

Resources within an organization are limited be it financial, human or physical, each manager is responsible for effectively allocating these resources to ensure they are used efficiently.

Managers may spend a lot of time as disturbance handlers, as conflicts arise, which is closely linked to negotiator. Managers must be good negotiators demonstrating and teaching the art of compromise.

Informational Roles:

Managers must monitor conditions inside and outside the organization so they are not blind-sided by change.

Organizations are responsible for communicating with their employees, customers and vendors. This role is accomplished by the role of a disseminator.

Functions of Management: as identified by Henri Fayol, 1916, in his book called general and industrial management, are: planning, controlling, organizing and leading.

Planning: This is a critical function that prepares an organization for the future by anticipating its needs and developing action plans to ensure that the organization reaches its goals. Without careful planning, an organization cannot meet its objectives.

Controlling: This function involves measuring actual performance and then comparing it to the expected (or planned) performance. Improving performance may mean training employee, transforming employees, hiring more talented applicants, changing job designs and so on.

Leading: With the demise of control & command manager, the ability to lead has become essential in managing human resources. The word "manager" is being changed with leader or coach. Leading is now more closely related to coaching and mentoring than commanding.

Managers today have less legitimate authority and must rely more on their personal power to effectively lead human resources.

The Role of Conceptual, Technical and Human Skills

According to Robert Katz, a working researcher in the 1970s suggested that a manager at all organizational level must possess conceptual, technical and human skills. The mix change as the worker progresses up the organizational hierarchy.

Conceptual skills: This is the ability to see or conceptualize the big picture, the ability to see beyond the immediate functional area in order to know how it works or fit into the overall organization.

People with conceptual skills are able to understand the inter-relatedness of an organization and also take into account the impact of the external environment on their company. It ensures that employees do not limit their perceptions to their department only (silo mentality) for any action taken will have a consequence in other departments.

Technical skills: These are skills required to perform more specialized tasks. These skills include technology, equipment, education and experience to perform a job. Acquiring such technical skills provides workers with more opportunities for advancement.

Human skills: These are skills for interaction with others. These skills are a crucial component of success today, with the demise of the command and control manager, and the global trend of a lateral organizational structure that involves interaction with peers.

Katz suggested that at lower management, 30% human skills, 50% technical. At middle management, more emphasis on conceptual (50%) than technical skills (30%). At top management level, 30% human, 50% conceptual and 20% technical.

Note that human skills at all levels remain relatively constant because interaction with others is critical at all levels.

Technical skills become less important as you move further away from operational people.

Conceptual skills become more important as the manager moves up the hierarchy, because it becomes more important to see the bigger picture. All managers should work to cultivate these skills. They can then adjust the mix as they move up in the organization.

Human resource manager competence

HR M must be competent in business

Have a thorough knowledge of human resource information, be able to manage, change and be trustworthy.

HR managers must understand the customers, changing customers' expectations and trends in the industry's environment e.g. technological changes to ensure that people with the appropriate skills are hired.

COMPENSATION: THEORY AND ADMINISTRATION

People all over the world engage in different activities for one purpose or the other. While engaged in these various activities like work, voting, marriages, and religion and so on, each and every individual expects some sort of benefit(s) from activities involved.

When you work, you expect some monetary payment/benefits that will allow you take care of your needs and wants. You also expect the president you have elected successfully through casting your vote to make all necessary amenities available for your country, thereby making life easier and more convenient. The wife you married is expected to take care of your home and children, while you are providing what it takes. The God which you worship in your religion to finally keep you in heaven not hell.

Historically, we all expect some sort of compensation for everything we engage in.

> Compensation is the sum total of all financial rewards and benefits provided by an organization in exchange for the employee's contribution. It is a reward system which reflects the employees' value to the firm.

> Compensation helps an organization retain and attract skilled employees.

> Employees are more motivated when they feel their contributions are fairly and equitably rewarded.

Wages and Salaries

In any country you go to, you find out that some people receive higher remuneration than others, despite the fact that the higher paid people look like they do less work.

That is the basic difference between wages and salaries. Wages are determined by the work, while salaries are determined by the job. For instance, a company executive and a security man working in the same organization.

Wages: These are usually hourly or daily rates paid by the amount of time worked. It is sometimes referred to as a "piece rate system", that is, you are paid for what you have produced (e.g. garment companies, brick producers, car wash etc).

Salaries: These are usually monthly or annual compensations. The actual time worked on the job is not a pay determinant. It is usually for the skilled professionals.

Internal equity and external equity

These issues need careful analysis by an organization, because it is a determinant of employee motivation in every industry, be it public or private.

> External equity has to do with an analysis whether to pay employees at market rates, below or above. Some organizations always pay higher in order to attract the best people in the field. However, it is also a determination of the size and performance of the organization.
>
> Internal equity is the establishment of pay levels in the organization that reflects worth of jobs. It usually compares knowledge, skills, abilities and responsibilities required to perform a job successfully.

BENEFITS

This is often referred to as an indirect compensation. This is because they are not expressed in monetary terms.

> Benefits are often used to attract employees and improve the satisfaction level of the workforce.
>
> There are required benefits due to employees by law, while there are also voluntary benefits, which have become so popular that employees feel they are entitled to them.

The required benefits employees must offer are social security, unemployment compensation and workers compensation.

Voluntary benefits include but not limited to childcare, pension plans, severance pay, and time off pay, wellness programs and insurance and so on.

PERSONNEL STAFFING AND EVALUATION

Every nation must plan. Plans must be made on how to utilize resources. Forecasts must be on and about every sector of a nation's affairs. The Army, Air force, Navy, Medical Doctors, Teachers, Lecturers, Civil Servants, Politicians and so on and so forth.

It is a fact that "he who fails to plan, plans to fail". No country, organization, family or individual can succeed without planning in order to achieve one goal or the other.

The politician has to plan in order to go about his campaign procedures and processes.

The teacher has to make his curriculum organized according to the syllabus so that knowledge can be impacted according to the planned sequence of study.

Human Resource Planning: This is the process of forecasting future human resource needs of an organization so that steps can be taken to ensure that these needs are met.

Human resource serves two purposes:

(i) **Setting goals and objectives:** Organizations need to specify where they want to be at some future point in time. This enables management and business planners to evaluate whether given goals can be realistically met.
(ii) **Examining the effects of alternative human resource policies and programs:** Organizations look at short and long run costs and arrive at the one that maximizes organizational effectiveness.

PERFORMANCE EVALUATION:

This is the collection and analysis of data relative to the behaviors of individuals.

Work has to be evaluated in order to recognize performance.

Productivity is vital for business management, thus, managers are keenly interested in maximizing work results, achieving program objectives and improving the quality of the work life for the employees.

Such assessments can be carried out periodically in order to give promotions, pay increase, demotion, or creation of training programs for development.

JOB ANALYSIS

Jobs are important to people in a lot of ways. It determines standard of living, residence status and even an individual's sense of worth.

It supersedes recruitment because there have to be some kind of determination of the kind of personnel required for each job and the specification of the number to be employed.

It studies the content of jobs to determine human requirements of the organization. This is done by collecting and analyzing information to the relevant job, like what the job seeks to accomplish, behavior required by the job, factors in the work environment, personal characteristics required to do the job e.g. qualification etc.

Job description is an analysis of overall tasks of a job.

Job specification is an overall summary of job requirements.

Job description and job specification make up job analysis.

RECRUITMENT AND SELECTION

Recruitment and selection have long run and short run impacts on an organization.

Employers must be quantity and quality conscious in order to create a committed workforce.

There should be tests and background reference checks to make the right choices.

Top management and line management are responsible and the relevant department should be competent to advice on whom to pick.

Topic Three

Marketing Management

People engage in a lot of exchanges in cash and kind everyday for one purpose or the other, either to satisfy their needs or for a particular purpose. Whichever way, no one can do without giving something in order to get something of seemingly higher priority at that moment. A market consists of all the potential customers sharing a particular need or want who might be willing and able to engage in exchange to satisfy that need or want. The size of a market depends on the number of people who exhibit the need or want and have the resources that interest others and are willing and able to offer these resources in exchange for what they want.

Markets see the sellers as the industry and buyers as the market.

The concept of a market brings about the concept of marketing. Marketing simply means working with markets to actualize potential exchanges for the purpose of satisfying human needs and wants.

Marketing Management: As defined by AMA, is the process of planning and executing the conception, pricing, promotion and distribution of goods/services and ideas to create exchanges that satisfy individual and organizational goals.

Marketing management takes place when at least one party to a potential exchange thinks about the means of achieving desired responses from other parties.

Marketing management can be practiced in any market, e.g. the purchasing manager has to plan purchase of raw materials, human resource manager has to deal with the labor market etc. They must therefore set objectives in order to achieve desired results in their various markets.

Marketing work in the customer market is formally carried out by sales managers, salespeople, customer service managers, marketing researchers etc. Each job carries well defined tasks and responsibilities. The popular image of the marketing manager is someone who creates or stimulates demand for the company's products; however this view is too limited of the diversity of marketing tasks performed by marketing managers.

Marketing management has the task of influencing the level, timing and composition of demand in a way that will help the organization achieve its objectives. It is essentially demand management.

Marketing managers manage demand by carrying out marketing research, planning, implementation and control. Within marketing planning, marketers must make decisions on target markets, market positioning, product development, pricing distribution channels, physical distribution, communication and promotion.

COMPANY ORIENTATIONS TOWARDS THE MARKET PLACE

Companies should have a guide towards achieving their organizational objectives like: what sort of marketing efforts, interests of the organization, the customers and the society at large.

Sometimes company interests may be conflicting e.g. favorable to customers but a hazard to the society.

There are five (5) competing concepts under which companies can choose to conduct their marketing activities as outlined by Kotler namely:

(i) **The production concept:** This concept holds that consumers will favor products that are widely available and in low cost. Companies using this concept concentrate on achieving high production efficiency and wide distribution. It is usually adopted when demand exceeds supply and also where products' price is high and has to be decreased to expand the market.

(iii) **The product concept:** Organizations that adopt this concept concentrate on making superior products and improving them over time. Under this concept, managers assume that buyers admire well made products and can appraise product quality and performance. Companies need to watch out not to get caught up in a love affair with their product and not realize the market is less turned-on, because they can easily forget customers' inputs trusting their engineers to design or improve and probably even forgetting to examine competitors products.

(iv) **The selling concept:** Companies that use this concept hold the view that, consumers if left alone will ordinary not buy enough of the company's products, so they must therefore undertake an aggressive selling and promotion effort. This concept is usually adopted by firms with overcapacity of products to sell rather than what the market wants.

(v) **The marketing concept:** This holds that the key to achieving organizational goals is by being more effective than competitors in integrating marketing activities toward determining and satisfying the needs and wants of target markets. This concept rests on four pillars: target market, customer needs, integrated marketing and profitability.

(vi) The societal marketing concept: Hold that the company's task is to determine the needs, wants and interests of target markets and to deliver the desired satisfactions more effectively and efficiently than competitors in a manner that preserves or enhances the consumers and the society's well-being. It calls upon companies to build social and ethical consideration into their marketing practices. They must find a balance in between the customers, the company profit and public interest.

Marketing Channels

Ralph Tresvant is a music artist that produces albums periodically for his fans. Now each time Ralph produces an album, he along with his firm have to find a way of letting the new album get to the fans, which means there have to be a channel to make that happen. Before a product reaches the consumer, it must pass through a chain of intermediaries, each passing the product down to the next organization.

Channels are important because consumption of any product/service is a function of availability. One can only consume products that are available.

Each of the elements in the chain has specific needs and performs different functions, which the producer must take into account, along with the requirements of the end user. Have you considered how a product from China is consumed in Nigeria? Or how Ralph's CD gets to Nigeria and other parts of the world?

Marketing Channel: Could be defined as a set of interdependent organizations involved in the process of making a product or service available for use or consumption.

Marketing channel decisions are one of the most critical decisions facing management. The channel chosen ultimately affects all other marketing decisions.

The electricity channel for example, is simple and almost ideal, the producer has mass distribution and the consumer has instant availability, at the nick of a switch. By contrast the channel for man-made fibers is more complex: the chain runs from spinners, dyers, weavers or knitters, garment manufacturers, retailers, until it finally reaches the consumer.

A distribution system takes years to build, and is not easily changed.

Work performed by marketing channels:

Many producers lack the financial resources to carry out direct marketing, which is very cumbersome and expensive. For example, Airtel Nigeria, a communications company, sells its products through more than 100 dealer outlets in the north of Nigeria alone.

In some cases, direct marketing is not feasible, e.g. a company selling gum will not find it easy to establish small retail gum shops throughout the world or sell through mail order. It will have to sell along with other small products and would end up in the drug store and grocery store business.

Producers who establish their own channels can often earn greater return, but intermediaries normally achieve superior efficiency in making goods available and accessible to target markets. They offer the firm more than what it can achieve on its own.

Channel Functions

A marketing channel moves goods from producers to consumers, and it overcomes the time, place and possession gaps that separate goods and services from consumers.

They place orders with manufacturers, gather information about potential and current customers, competitors and other actors and forces in the marketing environment.

They develop and disseminate persuasive communication to stimulate purchasing, assume risks associated with carrying out channel work, provide for successful storage and movement of physical goods and oversee transfer of ownership from one organization or person to another.

CHANNEL LEVELS:

A zero-level channel, also called a direct marketing channel, consisting of a manufacturer selling directly to a consumer.

A one-level channel contains one selling intermediary such as a retailer.

A two-level channel contains two intermediaries.

A three-level channel contains three intermediaries.

Channel levels can be longer depending on the peculiarity or complexity of a product or service.

Service Sector channel:
Schools develop "educational-dissemination systems" hospitals have to be located in good geographic areas to serve people, voting booths must be placed in wards so that ballots can be cast easily, barbing salons and restaurants all have to be strategically located for services rendered etc.

Channel Decisions
Choosing a channel is a major decision for most organizations because once an option is chosen or selected, it becomes difficult and expensive to make major changes.

If a company decides to make sales directly to the end user, there may be unacceptable cost penalties, and if one chooses to use the intermediaries, the amount of control that a producer has over the relationship with the end user can be significantly reduced.

Factors determining channel decisions:
The corporate strategy, product cost and consumer location

The characteristics of the channel must be in line with the overall requirements of the marketing strategy, e.g. ice fish needs to be kept refrigerated thus requires a very specialized distribution chain.

Where the end users are located and where they do their shopping has a major influence too.

Logistics Strategy

Every item, be it small or large in size has to go through some certain processes to be moved or relocated from one place to another.

Goods and services do not reach the target market without some sort of a distribution system.

The effectiveness of logistics will have a significant impact on both customer satisfaction and company costs.

A poor distribution system can destroy an otherwise good marketing effort. The right product with the right channel, advert etc.

Nature and importance of physical distribution and marketing logistics:

To some managers, physical distribution means trucks and ware houses only.

Modern logistics is much more than that.

Physical distribution or marketing logistics is the planning, implementing and controlling the physical flow of materials, final goods and related information from points of origin to points of consumption to meet customer requirements at a profit.

Traditional physical distribution typically starts with products at the plant and trying to find low-cost solutions to get it to customers while,

Marketing logistics thinking starts with the market place and works back to the factory. Logistics addresses the problem of outbound distribution (moving products from the factory to customers) and inbound distribution (moving, products & materials from suppliers to the factory).

It is the logistics manager's task to coordinate the whole channel of physical distribution system.

Companies today lay a lot of emphasis on logistics due to several reasons such as:

(i) Customer service and satisfaction has become the cornerstone of marketing strategy in many businesses, and distribution is an important customer service element.

(ii) Companies realize that they can win and keep customers with better service delivery through more effective logistics.

(iii) The more efficient the logistics, the cheaper the products and vice versa, because about 15% of a product's price is accounted for by shipping and transport alone.

(vi) Technology has brought about positive improvements in distribution efficiency.

MAJOR LOGISTICS FUNCTIONS

A company is expected, at all the time, to design a logistics system that will minimize the cost of attaining the company's objectives.

The major functions are:

(i) **Order processing:** Orders can be received through mail, telephone, sales peoples or via computer and electronic data interchange (EDI). Once received, orders must be processed quickly and accurately. Both the company and customers benefit when orders are carried out efficiently.

Computerized systems of order, shipping and billing are used now which reduces distribution costs and increased level of service to customers.

(ii) **Warehousing :** Companies need to store goods while they await orders, which mean storage facility is needed because consumption and production cycles rarely match.

(iii) **Inventory:** This could affect satisfaction. The main task is to maintain a balance between carrying too much stock or too little. Carrying too little may result in stock out, while carrying too much may result in heavy inventory costs.

(iv) **Transportation:** Choice of transportation affects the pricing of a product, thus the right choice needs to be made from rail, road, air, water or pipeline.

DESIGNING INTERNATIONAL DISTRIBUTION CHANNELS:

International marketers face many additional challenges in setting their international distribution systems.

Marketers (companies) must therefore adapt their channel strategies to the existing structures within each country.

Inbound and outbound supplies have now moved from domestic to global, hence the need for efficient distribution systems.

Integrated logistics management: This recognizes that providing better customer service and trimming down distribution costs requires teamwork both inside and outside the company (all the marketing channel organizations). The goal is to harmonize all of the company's distribution decisions. Use of IT and internet to develop electronic market places, which brings manufacturers and suppliers for online business (sourcing, raw materials, procurement, auctions and other services).

PROMOTIONAL CAMPAIGNS

When you are about to contest for the position of president of your class, the students union, or the president of your country, you usually have to stand in front of your classmates, colleagues or the public, and state the ideals which you stand for, what and how you intend achieve your programs, which in turn will earn you support from the people whom are supposed to vote for you.

Even when seeking a wife, you tend to engage in different ways of convincing the lady why she should accept you, why you are the ideal and perfect man for her.

As a matter of fact, we engage in promotional campaigns of all sorts in life, in order to achieve a certain goal or objective.

Countries showcase their potentials in different ways, indicating their potentials and capabilities, so that other countries know what they have and approach them for further transactions.

Goals and objectives would be cumbersome to achieve without the tools of promotional campaigns. Individuals, organizations and countries make aware of certain purposes, goals and objectives through promotional campaigns.

There are four distinct tools of promotional campaigns namely:

(i) Advertisement
(ii) Sales promotions
(iii) Personal selling
(iv) Public Relations

These tools are used in relation to the goals or objectives needed to be achieved.

Let us take a look at these tools:

(i) **Advertisement**
This has become an integral part of our society. It is a vital marketing and communication tool.

It is a "paid form" of message designed to make known what we have to buy or sell. It can sell goods, services, ideas and concepts when used through the right channels, methods and communication strategies.

All businesses require marketing. Politicians have to print and distribute posters and other publicity materials such as handbills, flyers etc showcasing their physical appearance and carrying their mandate. This will enable the public to be aware of whom to vote for or not, for progress enhancement.

This applies to other businesses as well. Companies have to make known their products and be persuasive, indicating the benefits of the products so that the public can reach out and buy.

Marketing is a system of business designed to plan, promote and distribute (goods and services) something of value to the benefit of the market, both present and potential household and industrial users.

You hardly can go through newspapers, radio, TV, billboards, buses, trains, stadium, matchboxes etc, without coming across one advert or the other aimed at making us aware of the advertisers' product(s).

Adverts mould our ideas towards products, services, ideas etc. Adverts are usually paid for and presented in a non-personal form, with an identified sponsor.

Advertisement could also be educative or persuasive, for example, promotion of accident free journey, protection measures towards AIDS and so on.

(ii) Sales Promotion

In a lot of situations, people are enticed with one form of reward or another when they achieve or attain a certain goal or objective. The Super Eagles of Nigeria were promised an extra bonus of ($) 80,000 dollars for every match they win at the 2010 South Africa World Cup. This was asides their normal mandatory expenses. Sometimes you promise your child a brand new bike when he assumes the first position in his class.

All these have one thing in common:—motivating, having something extra at the end of a particular act or event.

Sales promotion generally, is a temporary measure designed to boost sales for a specific period of time.

It creates that "extra something" that can generate enthusiasm and eventually boost the purchasing/action mood. It generally creates a feeling that you are getting a better deal and increases buying responses from consumers.

It also gingers selling efforts and can also attract new buyers/users. Sales promotion can be a powerful reinforcement for advertising and personal selling. Form of promotion could be through various methods depending on company strategies.

(iii) Personal Selling

Personal selling is an art that relies heavily on training and skills of an individual, who engages in persuasive communication.

This also applies to different spheres of life whereby one has to talk in order to convince and deliver his objective or goal. The politician aspiring to become a Governor will have to convince his people why they should choose him and not someone else, or why "lady X" should choose "Mr. B" as a husband instead of "Mr. Y", despite both of them being credible looking candidates for a future husband.

Eventually, the individual with a better overall presentation may become the preferred candidate.

Personal selling can always be targeted towards a larger potential customers and the salesman, whether a marketer, politician or potential husband can ask questions and receive answers immediately. The product can also be shown and demonstrated if necessary.

The most important aspect is its usefulness when it comes to custom made products.

(iv) Public Relations

This is often referred to as "PR". It encourages people to adopt a favorable attitude towards a company or individual as the case may be, that is doing some good for an industry or community and indirectly looks favorably towards its products too.

For example, people tend to value products of a company engaged in sponsoring the education of their children in a community than the other company that is not. The gubernatorial aspirant that has done a lot of humanitarian and philanthropic activities is likely to be a better choice of the people than the other self styled candidate the community has never benefited from.

In essence, you cannot do without some sort of promotional campaign in running your life, be it your finance, your family, your office or your country depending on the sphere applicable to you as an individual.

Retail Management

Retailing: Includes all the activities involved in selling goods and services directly to final consumers for their personal, non-business use. A retailer or retail store is any business enterprise whose sales volume comes from retailing, primarily.

Any organization that does this type of selling, whether a manufacturer, wholesaler or retailer—is doing retailing, irrespective of how or where the goods or services are sold, i.e. in store, on the street, in the consumer's home etc.

TYPES OF RETAILERS

Store retailing: This attracts a lot of customers because of the assorted products they offer. Consumers today can shop for goods and services in a wide variety of stores.

Like products, retail-store types pass through stages of growth and decline that can be described as the retail life cycle.

A retail store emerges, enjoys a period of accelerated growth, and reaches maturity and then declines.

Older retail forms took longer years to reach maturity, but newer ones reach maturity earlier.

Conventional retail-store-types typically offer many services to their customers and price their merchandise to cover the costs.

The higher cost of the bigger ones provides an opportunity for new store forms to emerge, e.g. discount stores which offer lower prices and lower services. As these discount stores increase their market share, they offer more services and upgrade their facilities, bringing an increase in their running costs, thereby making them vulnerable to newer types of low-cost stores.

Non-Store-Retailing: Non-store retailing has been growing faster than store retailing, amounting to a lot of consumer purchases. Observers predict that as much as half of general merchandise will be sold through non-store retailing by the end of the century. In fact some observers foresee as much as a third of all general merchandise retailing being done through non-store channels such as mail order shopping, TV and home computer shopping via the internet by end of the century.

Retail organizations: Although most retail stores are independently owned, an increasing number are falling under some corporate retailing.

Retail organizations achieve many economies of scale such as greater purchasing power, wider brand recognition and better trained employees.

Some major types of corporate retailing are chain stores, voluntary chains, retailer cooperatives, consumer cooperatives, franchise organizations and merchandising conglomerates.

Retailer Marketing Decisions: Today retailers are anxious to find new marketing strategies to attract and hold customers by offering a convenient location, special or unique assortments of goods, greater and better services than competitors, and store credit cards to enable purchase on credit.

Today many stores offer similar assortments.

In their drive for volume, the national and international manufacturers are now found in most departmental stores and other outlets, resulting into making retail stores and other retailers look more and more alike.

Service differentiation has also eroded. Many stores have trimmed their services, because customers have become smarter and more sensitive, not seeing a reason to pay more for identical brand, especially when services are diminishing, nor do they need to get credit from the store because bank credit cards have become universally accepted by all stores now.

For these reasons, many retailers are rethinking their marketing strategies e.g. departmental stores due to competition from discount houses and specialty stores are moving into the sub urban areas where there is ample parking space and families with purchasing power. Others are running more frequent sales, remodeling their stores and experimenting with mail order and telemarketing.

Facing competition from super stores, supermarkets are opening larger stores and carrying a larger number and variety of items and upgrading their facilities. They have also increased their promotional budgets and moved into private brands to reduce their dependence on national brands only and increase their profit margins.

Target Market Decisions: A retailer's most important decision concerns the target markets.

Whether the focus of the store should be focused on upscale, midscale or downscale shoppers is a decision to be made.

Do the shoppers want variety, assortment, depth or convenience?

Until the target market is identified, defined and profiled, the retailer cannot make consistent decisions on product assortment, store décor, adverts, price and so on.

Retailers that have not clarified their target-market and in trying to satisfy too many markets, end up satisfying none of them well.

Topic Four

GLOBAL MARKETING

Global marketing: The business environment is changing and organizations cannot ignore international markets. The world as a whole relies on each other for so many things required for livelihood. No country is an island of its own. You will notice that so many products consumed in your country are from other different countries. The increasing dependency of nations of the world on each other's goods and services has raised awareness among companies of the need for a more international outlook in their approach to business.

As their markets mature at home, the need to look for international markets arise so as to grow or keep growing.

Today, global competition is intensifying, because firms are aggressively looking into new international markets when home markets are no longer rich in opportunities. Local companies that never thought about competitors suddenly find them at their own backyards.

Firms that stay home to play safe not only miss the opportunity into new markets, but also risk losing its home market.

Some companies would like to stem the influx of foreign companies through protectionism, but in the long run, this would only raise the cost of living and protect inefficient firms.

Governments of various countries are placing more emphasis on foreign firms, such as joint ownership with local partners, hiring of nationals of the country and limiting profits that can be taken out of the country.

Global marketing is concerned with integrating or standardizing marketing actions across a number of geographic markets.

UNDERSTANDING THE GLOBAL ENVIRONMENT

A company must thoroughly research the international marketing environment before deciding whether or not to sell abroad.

The world economy has globalised, with world trade and investment having grown rapidly creating many attractive markets.

International trade has risen faster than the world output. The number of global companies has grown dramatically and the international financial system has become more complex and volatile.

THE INTERNATIONAL TRADE SYSTEM

Companies looking abroad must develop an understanding of the international trade system. Firms face various trade restrictions and challenges when selling to other countries, the most common is the tariff which may be designed to either raise revenue or protect domestic companies.

There may also be a quote limiting the amount of goods that can come into the country. A total ban on some kinds of products is the strongest form of quota.

Companies may also face non-tariff trade barriers such as biases against bids or restrictive product standards that favor or go against product features.

Certain forces like General agreement on Trade and tariff (GATT) also helps trade between nations because of certain tariff waivers imposed.

Each nation has unique features that must be understood, inclusive of its economic, political, legal and cultural environments.

DECIDING WHETHER TO GO INTERNATIONAL

Not all companies need to venture into the international markets to survive because companies going into the global market need to complete on a worldwide basis.

Several factors might draw a company into the international arena, thus:

(i) Global competitors might attack the company's home market by offering better products and lower prices. The company might want to counter attack these competitors in their home market to tie up their resources.

(ii) The company might discover markets with higher profit opportunities than their home market.
(iii) The company's domestic-market might be shrinking or stagnant, and they might need enlarged customer base in order to achieve economies of scale.
(iv) The company might want to reduce its independence on any one market so as to reduce its risk.
(v) The company's customers might be increasing abroad and require international servicing.

Before going abroad, a company must weigh several risks and answer on its ability to operate globally. Questions like: can it understand buyer behavior? Can it offer competitively attractive products? Will it be able to adopt the business cultures? Do the managers have the international experience? Has the management considered the impact of regulations and the political environments in other countries?

Due to the risks and difficulties of entering international markets, most companies do not act until some situation or event thrusts them into the global arena.

Topic Five

COMPUTER IN BUSINESS

You can only imagine what the fuel salesman will have to go through if he has to calculate the liters of fuel he sells to you off head. How does he quantify that he has sold off 15 liters to you? The same goes with your electricity bill, i.e. the amount and rate you have consumed in a month or a banker that has to calculate and balance all customer transactions at the end of the month? We all have to agree that it would not have been an easy task without the use of computers.

Literally, a computer is any device that is fed with data (input) works on the data (process) and brings out a result (output) as information.

These computers are found in different forms, basically three categories; (i) digital (ii) analogue (iii) hybrid

An example of a digital computer is the calculator or the desktop or laptop system. Analog computers can be found where volume is used like the filling station fuel pumping machine, while they hybrid computer is a combination of both.

COMPUTER IN BUSINESSES

Computers simply reduce tasks needing manual skills and strength. When properly applied, it can increase productivity.

The use of computers requires more problem solving skills and the ability to interpret data and is thus likely to lead to a widening gulf between skilled and unskilled workers.

Routine tasks requiring a low level of skill are fast disappearing from many business offices, e.g. manual typing is now replaced by word processors.

Computers have made it possible to combine jobs which were previously carried out separately and have also enabled lower level staff to carry out such functions, e.g. the telecommunications assistant can deal with a customer's query by directly assessing his account and solving his problems as they speak. Previously, such tasks were carried out by more than one person.

Computers have revolutionized how businesses are carried out in terms of ease, effectiveness and efficiency. It has made possible and available a lot of innovations in terms of business strategies and products in all fields of human business endeavor e.g.

Banking:	ATMs, online banking, electronic funds transfer
Manufacturing:	Industrial robots, CAD, CAM
Medicine:	Maintaining patient history, Endoscopy, Ultrasound, Sex detection at early pregnancy stage, Laser surgeries managing medical practice, medical research and training, credibility of medical training etc.
Government:	Election process, census etc.

IMPACT OF COMPUTERS ON ORGANIZATIONS

Computers alter the skill requirements for individuals and changes the way jobs are carried out. It can also alter the relationship between individuals and departments within the organization and even outside e.g. with customers and suppliers, i.e. transactions could be concluded through the use of computers.

Computers have a significant effect on the structure of organizations, making them flatter because top management can get to assess so many jobs taken by the middle management, thereby eliminating the middle management positions gradually in some organizations.

It could also create more jobs by creating new business opportunities and globalizing businesses. Businesses are being continuously reorganized into processes rather than functions.

Topic Six

COST MANAGEMENT SYSTEMS

COST OBJECT:

Mr. Ray is a businessman that travels to Dubai to buy goods and sell at his home in Nigeria. Whenever he embarks on such a trip, he writes down his ticket fare, feeding, accommodation and all other miscellaneous costs incurred, so that he could build it up into the goods in order to recover such expenses. A cost object is any activity for which a separate measurement of costs is desired. In other words, if users of accounting information want to know the cost of something, this something is called a cost object, e.g. the cost of a product, cost of rendering a service to a customer etc, cost of each of the item(s) imported, cost of rendering a service to a particular department or sales territory, or indeed anything for which one wants to measure the cost of resources used.

DIRECT COST AND INDIRECT COST OBJECTS

Direct costs: are costs that can be specifically and exclusively identified with a particular cost object.

Indirect cost: on the other hand, cannot be identified specifically and exclusively with a given cost object e.g. a furniture set manufactured by a company, in this situation the wood that is used to manufacture it can be specifically and exclusively referred to as a direct cost, with the wages of the operatives whose time can be traced to the specific desk are a direct cost. In contrast, the salaries of the factory supervisors, or rent of the factory cannot be specifically and exclusively traced to a particular desk and therefore classified as indirect costs.

Sometimes direct costs are treated as indirect costs e.g. the nails used in producing the furniture set.

Direct costs can be accurately traced because they can be physically identified with a particular object, whereas indirect costs cannot.

An estimate must be made of resources consumed by cost objects for indirect costs therefore, the more direct costs that can be traced to a cost object; the more accurate is the cost assignment.

Topic Seven

Entrepreneurship

The word entrepreneurship is a term with two words, "entrepreneur" and "ship".

'Entrepreneur' simply means a person who co-ordinates, manages, harmonizes, integrates and harnesses resources, while "ship" is the study.

Entrepreneurship is therefore defined as the study of a person who co-ordinates, manages, integrates, controls and harmonizes resources (non-human resources of materials, machinery, money method and marketing) to achieve organizational objectives.

>   The sociologist believes that entrepreneurship is governed by the society's value and status hierarchy and believes that entrepreneurship will flourish in a society where people depend on handiwork, initiation and good performance.

>   The psychologist opined the survival of a business is fundamentally based on individual personality traits, which drives the need for achievement, creativity, propensity to take risk, independence and leadership.

>   The economist maintained that entrepreneur is the fourth factor of production of land, labor and capital that

co-ordinate, harmonize and integrate the scarce resources to produce goods and services.

The anthropologists believed that an entrepreneur is the person with the characteristics of excellent humanitarian traits to go into the world of uncertainty.

The managers supported that an entrepreneur is somebody who combine the factors of production, plan, organize, motivate, direct, control and coordinate them to achieve organizational objective. Entrepreneur is therefore defined as the willingness and ability of an individual to seek out investment opportunities in an environment, and be able to establish and run an enterprise successfully based on the indentified opportunities.

FUNCTIONS OF THE ENTREPRENEUR

(i) Identification of an investment opportunity
(ii) Creativity
(iii) Risk bearing
(iv) Selection and acquisition of resources
(v) Establishing the enterprise

CHARACTERISTICS OF AN ENTREPRENEUR

(i) Self confidence
(ii) Risk taking
(iii) Result Oriented
(iv) Drive and energy
(v) Long term involvement
(vi) Leadership
(vii) Creativity

(viii) Taking initiative
(ix) Taking personal responsibility

SALARY EMPLOYMENT VERSUS ENTREPRENEURSHIP

Prospective managers or graduates face ultimate choice between salaried employment and entrepreneurship.

Salaried Employment: This usually involves job security because one is guaranteed a salary at certain periods such as weekly or monthly, which becomes certain, in contrast to a person managing his own job such as an entrepreneur who depends on profits.

Salaried employment ensures present and future securities in terms of pensions, super-remunerations, insurance, furniture, allowances, car and housing loans etc. It contains a certain degree of security.

PROBLEMS ASSOCIATED WITH SALARIED EMPLOYMENT

(i) Subordination
(ii) Transfer
(iii) Retirement
(iv) Lack of Initiative
(v) Wrong postings
(vi) Limited earnings

ADVANTAGES AND DISADVANTAGES OF ENTREPRENEURSHIP

The entrepreneur must come to terms with the facts of risks involved in entrepreneurship and its responsibilities. In this way, he gains satisfaction from his profits or returns and the prestige it brings him. The owner also finds satisfaction in using his abilities and creativity. He gains self respect and becomes his own boss, is free to take decisions, to take risks or opportunities. It provides great independence and the room to grow based on your initiatives and hard work.

Entrepreneurs offer opportunities for service in the community. Business ownership has the objective of profit expectation and profit gained from business is often greater than salary earned within a given period.

Thus, entrepreneurship is the way of satisfying life since it involves freedom and independence. The entrepreneur, however, is not sure when he will get his profits or gains from his business operations. He is not sure of tomorrow as far as risk is concerned and that is why he has less security compared with the salaried employee.

The entrepreneur may have more sense of pride and may have a more challenging career than the salaried employee. The salaried employee is also less worried than he who runs his own business, because the owner is always worried over logistics like working materials, funds for expansion, staff salaries etc. Thus it may not be right to say an entrepreneur enjoys more than the salary earner who not only enjoy paid leave grant but also long period rest. Above all, he has no risks like the owner of a business.

Thus it is always advisable that graduates or potential managers take jobs relevant to their fields in which to gain experience in that line before deciding on entrepreneurship. There is also the question of financial risk and personal career risk in entrepreneurship.

Topic Eight

FINANCIAL INSTITUTIONS, MARKETS AND ECONOMY

Financial System: A financial system is the catalyst of economic growth and development of a country.

The crucial role of the financial system can only be performed effectively and efficiently if the system is developed. This is the reason why the financial system is strictly controlled by the government and its agencies.

Financial systems vary among the economies of the world, with the most developed countries having more sophisticated financial systems while developing countries have growing financial systems. However, the actions and reactions of the developed financial systems have implications on the underdeveloped financial systems e.g. the poor housing loan recovery in the U.S.A that affected its economy and extended to other countries in the world.

A stable financial system is a pre-requisite for economic development of a nation.

Role of financial system: The role of financial system involves the entire macro-economic structure that gives responsibility to:

(i) Organize and sustain a sound payments mechanism

(ii) Intermediate funds between surplus and deficit units
(iii) Capital formation through monetary policy implementation.

The payments system consists of institutions, a set of instruments, procedures and communications systems employed to facilitate the discharge of financial obligations by agents. An efficient payment system ensures that financial transactions are effected with minimum delay and cost to the economy.

Financial Intermediation: means mobilizing and channeling of financial resources from the surplus spending to the deficit spending public for productive investment with a view to generating assets, instruments or securities in the process.

Monetary policy implementation has to do with and is dependent on a sound, efficient and stable financial system.

Financial markets: are those meeting places for people, corporations and institutions that either needs money to borrow or have money to invest.

Markets that focus on short-term securities are called "money markets" while those that focus on intermediate and long term securities are called capital markets.

Financial markets usually (i) shift funds from suppliers to users (ii) price securities (iii) liquefy securities (iv) discount the future, allocate funds and economic resources.

Assets are usually traded upon in terms of yield, maturity, marketability and risks.

Money markets: This is a place where money is traded. The money market is established primarily for the localization of a credit base in an economy.

It creates local investment outlets for retention of funds within an economy and also for the investment of funds that are usually taken out of the economy. It is an essential step on the path of economic development and independence.

The market is characterized by low-risk and highly short term debt instruments.

Players in the market include discount houses; deposit money banks, micro finance banks etc, and instruments include treasury bills, treasury certificates, commercial papers etc.

Capital markets: This market provides the intermediate and long term facilities for borrowing funds.

It provides funds for the implementation of government's capital projects and for establishment, expansion and modernization of businesses.

It provides a base for liquefying and allocating the scarce resources of a given economy.

It controls the granting of a quotation on the stock exchange.

It investigates any irregularities or alleged irregularities in dealings between members with their clients.

It promotes, supports and proposes legislative measures.

The market is composed of institutions like BOI, issuing houses, SEC, stock exchange houses etc.

Topic Nine

FINANCIAL REPORTING

Financial management: At the end of the month, when you are paid your salary, you sit and map out a budget: electricity bill, water bill, gas, groceries, mortgage, cinema, fuel for the car, kids' demands etc. You sort of prioritize your never ending needs and demands in order to be able to manage your income. You simply have to have a game plan to be able to make ends meet and not end up borrowing and running into financial problems. All in all, you have to adopt some sort of financial planning and management of your life in relation to your income, we all concur to this right? Financial management is simply the management of "raw money" available to an individual or firm and effective utilization of the raw money.

Cash is the most liquid asset of a firm and is more susceptible to stealing.

Companies and organizations encounter problems of fraud by some employees that indulge in stealing. In order to curtail stealing, the owner of a business should manage his finances efficiently.

Management of cash: This is the management of monies of a firm in order to attain maximum cash availability and maximum interest income.

This entails making cash available when needed (at the right time and quantity) and investing idle funds so as to have maximum possible returns on them.

Cash management may not be as simple as conveyed, because it involves the ability of the entrepreneur to be able to reach equilibrium in profitability and liquidity. There is always a tradeoff between the two.

It is always the desire of every company to be profitable and liquid at all times. The way we manage cash, if not properly done, will affect one negatively at the expense of the other.

However, inadequate cash means low liquidity, which could affect a firm's ability to effect maturing obligations and the firm's operations.

The level of cash a firm should maintain at a given time depends on the operations of the organization. That will be subject to the CEO of the company.

REASONS FOR HOLDING CASH

Three reasons have been identified for holding cash, thus:

(i) Transaction motive (ii) Precautionary motive (iii) Speculative motive.

(i) **Transaction motive:** Every business spends money on a daily basis to keep the business going such as payment of salaries, purchase of office stationery, postage, and electricity bills etc. The transaction motive for keeping cash therefore is for the company to meet its daily transactions and other needs.

(ii) **Precautionary motive:** Apart from the money kept for transaction purpose, it is also advisable for a company to keep cash to meet unexpected payments such as breakdowns of some machines or accidents etc.

(iii) **Speculative motive:** There may be need for an organization to hold cash for the purpose of taking advantage of any profitable opportunity that may prevent itself. In such a situation, the company feels it will make high returns for the company.

Topic Ten

INTERNATIONAL REAL ESTATE

INTERNATIONAL OVERVIEW

As investors expand their overseas activities and investments, appraisers are increasingly called upon to prepare appraisal reports in foreign countries for clients.

Domestic investors are accustomed to receiving appraisal reports that include subjects of local market dynamics.

To ensure correct market analysis abroad, appraisers usually consult with local appraisers in that particular country. Although the same principles are applied in valuation assignments throughout the world, local customs and institutions vary significantly.

The appraiser has to take cognition of these variances so as to be able to know the process involved, like taxes to be paid, implication of change of ownership and so on.

There also exist a body known as "international-real-estate-society", where appraisers join as members so as to get benefits of the global cooperation.

Ahmed Shehu Awak, PhD

GLOBALIZATION OF REAL ESTATE PRACTICE

The advent of technology has no doubt brought about tremendous improvement and greater efficiency in every aspect of human Endeavour. This feat has made globalization a reality, even in the aspect of real estate.

Globalization of real estate has brought about a better understanding of the various foreign laws, customs and land market behaviors in different parts of the world for easier real estate transactions as demanded by the new global village. Real estate firms now cross borders to find new markets in other countries with potentials to invest in real estate construction and businesses. This expansion is a positive phenomenon for the industry, for instance a real estate firm from Malaysia came into FCT Abuja, Nigeria, and built a 1000 housing unit estate and is reselling to individuals due to the market viability and demand. This is made possible due to globalization of the industry.

Today, you could buy a property anywhere in the world via the internet. Cross border investment in facilities and infrastructure investment also enhances international real estate transactions.

Topic Eleven

MANAGEMENT ACCOUNTING

INTRODUCTION TO MANAGEMENT ACCOUNTING:

Management Accounting describes accounting as the process of identifying, measuring and communicating economic information to permit informed judgments and decisions by users of the information.

In other words, accounting is concerned with providing both financial and non-financial information that will help decision makers take good decisions.

An understanding of accounting therefore requires an understanding of the decision-making process and an awareness of the users of accounting information.

USAGE OF ACCOUNTING INFORMATION

Accounting is a language that communicates economic information to people who have an interest in an organization, such as managers, shareholders, potential investors, employees, creditors and the government.

Managers require information that will assist them in their decision-making and control e.g. selling prices, costs, demand etc.

Shareholders require information on the value of their investment and the income derived from their shareholding. Employees require information on the ability of the firm to be able to pay their wages. Creditors and providers of loan require information on a firm's ability to meet its financial obligations. Inland Revenue requires information on the amount of profits that are subject to taxation. All these information is important for determining policies to manage the economy.

Accounting information is not confined to business organizations alone. It is also used by individuals and other bodies e.g. mosques, churches, and clubs and so on. Government units also require accounting information in order to report the results of their activities.

The objective is to provide sufficient information to meet the needs of the various users at the lowest possible costs.

Topic Twelve

PORTFOLIO MANAGEMENT

This field covers why people seek investments.

Why do people seek investments? The simple answer is in order to achieve an organized and secure living, so that when one is retired he/she will have something to fall back on to and to probably secure the future of one's offspring.

Investment defined: It is the setting aside or spending money for future financial gain. For an individual, investment might include the purchase of financial assets such as stocks, bonds, mutual funds, life insurance, houses or cars.

Economists refer to investments as increase in real capital in an economy, such as increase in factories and machinery or human capital, i.e. skilled and educated labor force.

Stock: This is a share of ownership in a corporation. These shares could be bought or sold, usually on a public stock exchange. Owners of stock could make a profit or capital gain if the stock is sold at a higher price than it was originally purchased.

Some companies enable stockholders to share in the profits of the company. Such payments to stockholders are referred to as "dividends".

Shareholders are also entitled to a share in the sale of the company if dissolved. They may also vote in person or by proxy on a variety of corporate affairs. Stockholders have a priority of buying more shares before it is offered for public sale and usually receive reports about the corporation's business performance.

Stocks are generally negotiable, that is it can be transferred from one individual to another.

A stockholder has the protection of limited liability which means he is not personally liable for the company's debts.

Why do corporations issue stock?

They issue stock majorly to finance their business activities. This option of raising funds is only available to corporations, not sole proprietorships or partnerships.

Why people buy stock

People buy stock for economic gains either as dividends and/or appreciation from stock purchased.

In terms of financial claim against a company, bonds are safer investments than stocks in terms of deflation, while stocks are better in terms of inflation.

Bonds are also available to sole proprietors and partnerships. In the issuance of a bond, the company promises to pay periodic interest and pays back the initial loan after expiry of the agreed period thus bonds are evidence of loans, while stocks are evidence of ownership.

Corporations that have Initial Public Offerings (IPO) are usually young companies in need of large amounts of capital. A company can only have one IPO, the first time it makes stock available to the public. Others are referred to as subsequent offering for further business development.

Privately owned corporations do not go public, mainly not to share their profits or not to lose control of the corporation.

Investment decisions: This often involves and requires substantial amounts of money. Many of such decisions are also difficult to reverse and can affect business far into the future.

A business regards an investment as successful if it increases the wealth of a company.

This is accomplished when the firm earns profits and passes it to shareholders either as dividends or as increase in the value or price of the stock.

Profits or earnings not distributed to shareholders are referred to as "retained earnings".

In taking an investment decision, consideration is given to what project to invest into, based on two criteria:

(i) Expected rate of return, and
(ii) Risk or uncertainty of achieving the expected rate of return

RAISING MONEY FOR INVESTMENTS

(i) **By paying smaller dividends:** a firm can raise more funds by paying out smaller dividends so as to increase its retained earnings and use it for investments. This method appeals to managers because they can avoid paying interest.
(ii) **By borrowing:** a firm may choose to borrow money to fund its projects, either from a bank or by issuing bonds. It will pay interest if it borrows money, but it can deduct the interest from its profits and therefore pay less tax. However, there are limits to borrowing, if it borrows too much, it could lead to bankruptcy.
(iii) **By selling more stock:** these are funds that belong to the company and do not have to be repaid thereby eliminating any expenses of paying interest. The firm must however still earn a certain return on its investment to obtain cash to pay dividend or devote to retained earnings.

Businesses may still face the costs of issuing stock such as fees for legal and banking services, which are usually higher than for issuing bonds.

MANAGING RISKS

Events outside the corporation can affect the firm and its financing decisions e.g. a change in interest rate can suddenly make borrowing very in expensive or costly. Land rate hike can make buying of real estate very expensive.

Topic Thirteen

LABOUR MANAGEMENT RELATIONS

Industry in a general sense is the production of goods and services in an economy. The term industry refers to a group of enterprises, private or government-operated that produce a specific type of good or service e.g. beverage industry, automotive industry etc.

Some industries produce physical goods (e.g. cars), while others provide services (e.g. airlines), others are banking, restaurants etc.

The word industry is Latin which means "diligence" which reflects the highly disciplined way human energy, natural resources and technology are combined to produce goods and services in an economy.

INDUSTRY CLASSIFICATIONS

An industry is usually classified by the major input or by the final product e.g. when the final product is used by another industry, it is called a producer good, when the final product is used by people, it is called consumer goods.

Primary industries: use raw resources as major inputs e.g. agriculture, mining, fishing etc.

Tertiary industries: provide services e.g. banks, universities, retail stores etc.

Labor: simply refers to workers as a group. Workers in an industry sell their own labor in exchange for an income they negotiate with the management.

Negotiations may occur on an individual basis, many wage negotiations occur between management and employees who have organized groups called labor unions.

Relationship between management and labor often involve serious conflicts, while labor may be requesting for higher wages to improve their standard of living, management may resist because it may cut into profits.

Management: simply refers to getting things done through others. Managers supervise, monitor and coordinate the different areas of an industry.

Natural resources: Natural resources play a critical role in industrial growth.

There are renewable natural resources that regenerate over time, e.g. Agric-land, fisheries etc.

There are non-renewable natural resources that do not regenerate or termed as fixed, e.g. mineral resources.

Collective Bargaining: This is the negotiation between employers and employees (who are usually represented by a labor union) about terms and conditions of employment.

The bargaining process is usually concerned with wages, working hours and fringe benefits, job security, safety and other working conditions. One or more of these may be the subject of consideration.

Sometimes private mediators and government officials may be involved especially when a major industry is involved.

Labor union: refers to an association of workers that seek to improve the economic and social well-being of its members through group action. It represents its members in negotiations with an employer.

Types of Unions

(i) **Craft unions:** organized workers employed in the same occupation or craft, regardless of where they work. E.g. unions of electricians, mechanics, taxi drivers.

(ii) **Industrial union:** organizes all workers in an industry, regardless of the workers crafts. E.g. auto-unions, steel etc.

Topic Fourteen

MULTINATIONAL BUSINESS FINANCE

MULTINATIONAL BUSINESS FINANCE:

Various parties to international business must be able to exchange currencies of one country with that of another in order to facilitate trade and investments.

The currency conversions however could be speculative or protective. Speculative in the hope of making profits or protective in order to lock in profits already made.

Parties involved include individuals, businesses, commercial banks and governments.

There are various rules and processes that govern and guide currency conversion.

FOREIGN EXCHANGE MARKETS AND PARTICIPANTS

A foreign exchange market provides as mechanism for transferring the money from one country to another.

Because of its close connection with the money, capital and other financial markets, it also serves as a means of supplying credit for and arranging the financing of international economic transactions.

The exchange markets are so well integrated that they together constitute a single world market, despite distance and time differences.

Foreign exchange transactions go hand in hand with import and export of goods and capital, hence many countries impose legal restrictions upon the amount and kind of trading allowed. Countries have to protect their domestic industries thus disallowing some certain kinds of importation into the country and exportation as well.

THE (IMF) INTERNATIONAL MONETARY FUND IN MULTINATIONAL BUSINESS FINANCE

The IMF system serves to assure maximum exchange—rate stability, and yet facilitates orderly changes when needed thereby avoiding competitive devaluations.

When joining the IMF, a country pays a subscription quota, 2.5% of which is due in gold and 7.5% in a country's own currency based on some certain criteria related to the size of the country and its national income.

This quota also determines a country's voting power in the fund and amount of foreign exchange it may draw. A country can withdraw at any point, to the amount of its subscription in gold, i.e. (2.5%).

Any country that wants to withdraw above its gold-trencher (2.5%) must have fund approval and only be used for remedying the country's balance of payments difficulties, and such withdrawal is limited to 200% of a country's quota.

The IMF's leverage over member countries is its ability to grant or deny access to funds and the fund membership qualifies membership with the World Bank.

THE WORLD BANK IN MULTINATIONAL BUSINESS FINANCE

The representatives that gathered for the Breton Woods Conference had two objectives in restructuring the International monetary system, thus:

(i) To promote international stability of currency and eliminate exchange restrictions, and
(ii) To provide assistance for post war reconstruction and development.

   The World Bank is referred to as "World Bank Group" because it has two affiliates namely: the International Development Association, and the International Finance Corporation.

   The World Bank is presently the major Public International Institution for source of financing. Its capital stock is owned by member countries and its primary source of funds is the private capital markets.

The Bank deals mainly in long term loans to member countries for specific development or reconstruction projects. It also lends to private projects if the Government endorses and guarantees the loan.

The World Bank is more important to international business as a general force for economic development than as a direct source for financing. The Bank has however expanded its activities since the late 60s, hence:

(i) The International Finance Corporation (IFC) in response to the need for a specialized international body to stimulate private enterprise and private investment in developing countries, now finances business projects mainly in the manufacturing and processing fields, through loans or equity participation without Government guarantees and endorsements. It provides a multinational source for financing international enterprise, but has not really played a great role in influencing international business environment.
(ii) The International Development Association (IDA) is focused towards providing soft-loans, i.e. loans with long maturity and relatively low-interest rates and easy payment terms to the less developed countries.

CENTRAL BANKS IN MULTINATIONAL BUSINESS FINANCE

The Central Bank of any country has a primary obligation of maintaining an efficient monetary system that encourages domestic growth without inflation. This internal objective is often affected by external forces. Central Banks may be forced to intervene actively in the external economic spheres in order to protect and attain domestic goals, so they often have a strong influence of foreign exchange markets.

Central Bank dealings in foreign exchange are undertaken to maintain orderly markets for the respective currencies thereby fostering or enhancing international trade and investment. Each Central Bank acts according to the peculiarity of its domestic goals and interests.

Topic Fifteen

ORGANIZATION AND MANAGEMENT PROCESS

The friendlier your work environment, the more conducive your workplace, the more accommodating the nature of relationship between a boss and subordinates, the smoother and more efficient and effective an organization will turn out. There is something of a revolution occurring in how organizations are structured now. Companies are doing away with the old organizational charts and experimenting with new designs that will hopefully improve coordination, sharing knowledge, and employee focus on critical objectives.

Organizational structure refers to the division of labor as well as the patterns of coordination, communication, work flow, and formal power that direct activities. An organizational structure reflects culture and power relationships. Knowledge of this subject provides the tools to engage in organizational design, that is, to create and modify organizational structures.

The two fundamental processes in organizational structure are: division of labor and coordination. The four main elements of organizational structure are: span of control, centralization, formalization and departmentalization.

DIVISION OF LABOR AND COORDINATION

All organizational structures include two fundamental requirements: the division of labor into distinct tasks and the coordination of that labor so employees are able to accomplish common goals. Recall that organizations are groups of people who work interdependently toward some purpose.

To efficiently accomplish their goals, these goals typically divide the work into manageable chunks, particularly when there are many different tasks to perform. They also introduce various coordinating mechanisms to ensure that everyone is working effectively toward the same objectives.

Division of Labor: Refers to the subdivision of work into separate jobs assigned to different people. Subdivided work leads to specialization, because each job now includes a narrow subset of the tasks necessary to complete the product or service.

Tasks are also divided vertically, such as having supervisors coordinate work while employees perform the work.

Job incumbents can master their tasks quickly because work cycles are very short. Less time is wasted changing from one task to another. Training costs are reduced because employees require fewer physical and mental skills to accomplish the assigned work. Job specialization makes it easier to match people with specific aptitudes or skills to the jobs for which they are best suited.

COORDINATING WORK ACTIVITIES

As soon as people divide work among themselves, coordinating mechanisms are needed to ensure that everyone works in concert. Every organization, from the two-person corner convenience store to the largest corporate entity, uses one or more of the following coordinating mechanisms: informal communication, formal hierarchy and standardization.

Informal Communications: is a coordinating mechanism in all organizations. This includes sharing information on interdependent tasks as well as forming common mental models so that employees can synchronize work activities using the same mental road map. Informal communication permits considerable flexibility because employees transmit a large volume of information through face-to-face communication and other media-rich channels. It is a vital coordinating mechanism in non-routine and ambiguous situations.

FORMAL COMMUNICATION:

Informal communication is the most flexible form of coordination, but it can be time consuming.

As organizations grow, they develop a second coordinating mechanism in the shape of a formal hierarchy. Hierarchy assigns legitimate power to individuals, who then use this power to direct work processes and allocate resources. In other words work is coordinated through direct supervision.

Any organization with an informal structure coordinates work to some extent through the formal hierarchy.

The formal hierarchy has traditionally been applauded as the optimal coordinating mechanism for large organizations. Coordination through formal hierarchy may have been possible with classic organizational theorists, but it is often a very inefficient coordinating mechanism. There are limits to how many employees a supervisor can coordinate. Furthermore, the chain of command is rarely as fast or accurate as direct communication between employees. Recent scholars have warned that today's educated and individualistic workforce is less tolerant of rigid structures and legitimate power.

Coordination through standardization: Creating routine patterns of behavior or output. Many organizations standardize work activities through job descriptions and procedures. This coordinates work requiring routine and simple tasks, but not in complex and ambiguous situations. In these situations, companies might coordinate work by standardizing the individual's or team's goals and product or service output.

When work activities are too complex to standardize through procedures or goals, organizations often coordinate work effort by extensively training employees or hiring people who have learned precise role behaviors from educational programs.

ELEMENTS OF ORGANIZATIONAL STRUCTURE:

The division of labor and coordination of work represent the fundamental requirements of organizations. These requirements relate to four basic elements of organizational structure: span of control, centralization, formalization and departmentalization.

(i) **Span of control:** refers to the number of people reporting directly to the next level in the hierarchy.
(ii) **Centralization:** means that formal decision authority is held by a small group of people, typically those at the top of the organizational hierarchy. But as organizations grow and become more complex with branches of operation all over regions or countries, the organization is decentralized, i.e. authority and power is disposed throughout the organization.
(iii) **Formalization:** This is the degree to which organizations standardize behavior, through rules, procedures, formal training and related mechanisms. It represents standardization as a coordinating mechanism e.g. McDonalds, Mr. Biggs, Banks etc.
(iv) **Departmentalization:** Specifies how employees and their activities are grouped together. It is a fundamental strategy for coordinating organizational activities because it influences organizational behavior in terms of establishment of a system of common supervision between positions and units within the organization. It also establishes formal work teams and also determines which positions and units must share resources, thus establishing interdependencies between employees and subunits.

Topic Sixteen

ORGANIZATIONAL BEHAVIOUR

Mr. Nas, being the boss in the organization could always tell "Mary had a bad night; John woke up on the wrong side of the bed today, "hey! Jay, take the day off today. Mr. Nas could like always detect the state of his staff, because he obviously took his time to understand the people around him helping him achieve his organizational goals. This means that human beings are not the same in terms of composition and one has to be able to monitor and understands such swings when he is around people. Organizational Behavior (OB) is the study of what people think, feel and do in and around organizations. Organizational behavior researchers systematically study individual, team and structural characteristics that influence behavior within organizations. Through research, scholars try to understand and predict how these behaviors help organizations succeed.

By saying that organizational behavior is a field of study, it means that scholars have accumulated and still accumulating a distinct knowledge about behavior in organizations.

ORGANIZATION:

An organization is a group/any group of people who work interdependently toward some purpose.

Organizations are not buildings or other physical structures, rather, they are people who work together to achieve a set of goals. Employees have structured patterns of interaction, meaning that they expect each other to complete certain tasks in a coordinated way and in an organized way.

THE NEED TO STUDY ORGANIZATIONAL BEHAVIOR

The main reason for studying Organizational Behavior is that most people work in organizations, so there is need to understand, predict and influence the behaviors of others in organizational settings. People in different fields of marketing, computer science, engineering, medicine etc have learnt different concepts of their various fields, but everyone needs organizational behavior knowledge to address the people issues he/she faces when trying to apply marketing, computer science or any other ideas. Everyone wants to know about the world in which we live in. This also applies to organizations, because they have a huge effect on our lives. We want to understand why organizational events occur and to more accurately predict what to expect in future.

The field of organizational behavior uses scientific research to help us understand and predict organizational life. Although 'organizational behavior' is not a perfect science, it helps us to predict what people will do under various conditions in organizations.

Whether you are a marketer or an architect, you need to know how to communicate effectively with others, manage conflict, make better decisions, build commitment to your ideas, and help work teams operate more effectively and so on.

"OB" concepts and theories will help you to influence organizational events. Although it takes a prescriptive view, it does so in the context of theory and research. It uses scientific research to build strong theory that provides the foundation for effective practice.

"OB" knowledge is for everyone not just managers. Indeed, as organizations reduce layers of management and delegate more responsibilities to other staff, the concepts of "OB" become more important for anyone who works in and around organizations. Therefore, the need to master the knowledge and skills required to influence organizational events becomes more inherent. That is why the emphasis is less on managing people. Of course organizations will continue to have managers but their roles have changed and, more important, the rest of us are now expected to manage ourselves.

THE FIVE ANCHORS OF ORGANIZATIONAL BEHAVIOR (OB)

To understand globalization, the changing work force, new employment relationship, computer technologies, work teams, business ethics, other topics and beliefs or knowledge structures of "OB", the five (5) conceptual anchors need to be known, because they represent the way that OB researchers think about organizations and how they should be studied. Let's take a peep into these 5 beliefs that anchor the study of OB:

(a) **The multidisciplinary anchor:**
    As part of the social sciences, OB is anchored around the idea that it should draw knowledge from other disciplines rather than just its own isolated research base, that is, it should be multidisciplinary. The fields of

psychology and sociology have contributed the most to current OB knowledge; the field of psychology has aided understanding of individual and interpersonal behavior. Sociology has contributed to the knowledge of team dynamics, organizational socialization, organizational power and other aspects of the social system.

Anthropology has mainly helped us to understand organizational culture, whereas political science contributed ideas regarding power and politics in organizations, economics on organizational power and decision making, and the communications field is currently helping us understand the dynamics of electronic mail, communicating corporate culture and socialization process.

(b) The scientific method anchor:
For the most part, OB researchers test their hypothesis about organizations by collecting information according to the scientific method. The scientific method is not a single procedure for collecting data; rather it is a set of principles and procedures that help researchers to systematically understand previously unexplained events and conditions.

(c) The contingency anchor:
"It depends" is a phrase that OB scholars often use to answer a question about the best solution to an organizational problem. The statement may sound frustrating to some people, yet it reflects an important way of understanding and predicting organizational events, called the contingency approach. This anchor states that a particular action may have different consequences in

different situations. In other words, no single solution is best in all circumstances.

(d) The multiple levels of analysis anchor:
Organizational events are usually studied from three common levels of analysis; individual, team and organizational. The individual level looks at the characteristics and behaviors of employees as well as the processes, attitudes and values. The team level of analysis looks at the way people interact, which includes team dynamics, decisions, power, organizational politics, conflict, and leadership. At the organizational level, focus is put on how people structure their working relationships and on how organizations interact with their environments.

For instance, communication includes individual behaviors and interpersonal (team) dynamics. It also relates to the organization's structure. In essence, one should look into each OB topic at the individual, team and organizational levels, not just one of the levels.

Systems as interdependent parts: Organizations have many interdependent parts, referred to as subsystems that must coordinate with each other in the process of transformation of inputs to outputs. These subsystems may include things like communication and reward systems, task activities like production and marketing, and power dynamics.

Organizational decision makers need to monitor these subsystems to ensure that they are aligned with each other and with the external environment.

Therefore, all employees need to anticipate new changes in one subsystem that affects other subsystems, and as organizations become larger, they develop more subsystems, and relationships between them become more complex. Subsystem interdependencies are so complex that an event in one department may ripple through the organization and affect other subsystems. It is important to make employees aware of this so as to minimize unintended consequences.

Knowledge management: Develops an organization's capacity to acquire, share and utilize knowledge in ways that improve its survival and success.

It provides a foundation for a stronger learning capability, generating a number of learning opportunities, generalizing the learning beyond the individual to others across the organization and building a motivation and opportunity to learn from others.

Brains have replaced brawls as the primary source of corporate wealth creation. Organizations gain more competitive advantage in the external environment through knowledge management; that is by effectively acquiring, sharing and utilizing knowledge.

Intellectual capital: This is the knowledge that resides in an organization. Intellectual capital is the sum of an organization's human, structural and customer capital.

Human capital is the knowledge that employees posses and generate, including their skills, experience and creativity. Structural capital is the knowledge captured and retained in an organization's system and structures.

Customer capital is the value derived from satisfied customers, reliable suppliers, and other external sources that provide added value for the organization.

The main source of an organization's competitive advantage is its intellectual capital.

Knowledge management process: Develop an organization's capacity to acquire, share and utilize knowledge so as to survive and succeed. This is often referred to as "organizational learning" because companies learn about their internal and external environments in order to survive and succeed through adaptation. The "capacity" to acquire, share and utilize knowledge means that companies have established systems, structures and organizational values that support the knowledge management process.

Knowledge acquisition: This is the organization's ability to extract information and ideas from its environment as well as through insight.

Knowledge sharing: This is the ability of organizations to effectively disseminate knowledge acquired. Many organizations are reasonably good at acquiring knowledge but waste this resource by not effectively disseminating it. Recent studies have shown that knowledge sharing is usually the weakest link in knowledge management. Most of the time, valuable ideas sit idly, just like unused inventory. Formal training is useful, but most sharing occurs through communication processes that quickly and fluidly share meaningful information across organization boundaries.

Teams also play an important role in knowledge sharing. Organizations disseminate knowledge by seeding teams with new members who bring in valuable experience from successful teams in the past.

Knowledge utilization: Any knowledge acquired and shared is wasted, unless it is effectively put to use. This means making sense of the information received and applying it to employee behaviors whether directly or through organizational systems and structures.

Employees need to realize that they possess information to potentially improve customer service or product quality, which requires clear role perceptions. They must be able to make sense of the information they receive, and need to have the freedom to apply their knowledge. Thus, knowledge utilization requires employee empowerment.

Organizational memory: Simply refers to the storage and preservation of intellectual capital. This includes information employees possess as well as knowledge embedded in an organization's systems and structures. It includes documents, objects, and anything else that provides meaningful information about how the organization should operate. Organizational memory could be looked upon as the stock of knowledge an organization possess at any given time.

Topic Seventeen

PRODUCTION PLANNING AND CONTROL

Production: This is generally the process by which goods and services are made available for the economy as a whole. This could be houses, cars, foods, clothes, drinks etc.

There has to be a proper way or method of production. You don't first decide to produce an egg, e.g. you have to rear the chicks and specifically a "layer" breed before it can be achieved.

All production function of an organization exists solely to make available goods and services for customers.

Production management: Is concerned with the provision of goods. It is the central part of the manufacturing process, which shoulders the responsibility of planning, resourcing and controlling the processes involved in converting raw materials and components into finished goods in order to satisfy the needs and wants of the organization's existing and potential customers.

Modern production processes are usually complex and costly, with machines, computers and materials of all kinds and labor, all have to be blended together to enable the production system carry out its operations in a cost effective way. Thus production processes require careful planning and control.

Purchasing (Procurement): This is an important aspect of production management because purchasing cost represents a substantial part of the total cost of production.

An effective and efficient cost purchase can make all the difference between a company's product and that of its competitors.

The primary responsibility of the purchasing/procurement department is to ensure sufficient and suitable raw materials. Components and other goods/services required for the manufacturing process in a cost effective manner.

Purchasing decisions are very important and risky to an organization because it can easily affect product prices.

It has been estimated that a 5% increase or excess in purchasing costs can lead to a 25% reduction in profits. Therefore a small saving in purchasing costs can be worth more to an organization.

Material request planning: Is an internal production process designed to ensure that materials are available when required,

The process is closely linked to production planning and purchasing which provide the context for material request planning decisions.

Once set up, the process lends itself to computerization, which enables other functions like ordering and purchasing to be linked into the system.

Just in time (JIT) systems: This represents a good step forward from MRP, because unlike material request planning, the materials arrive just when needed, not before or after but just in time.

In theory, it leads to no stock being held, and in practice it minimizes them.

JIT requires total commitment from the workforce and its suppliers. No room for errors is required and it works best in a stable production environment. It reduces manufacturing time, increases equipment utilization, simplifies planning and scheduling, improves quality and reduces scrap and wastage.

This method has been used with great success by large Japanese firms and is being widely adopted by firms all around the world.

This system is however not easy to implement because of its demand on the planners workforce and suppliers.

Inspection: This has to do with quality control. The control starts with the inspection of raw materials and other items purchased, continue with inspection during production and ends with final inspection before delivery to the customer.

The basic reasons for inspection are:

(i) To accept or reject items
(ii) To control the whole production process
(iii) To improve the process if necessary

Maintenance: This is the work undertaken to keep or restore every facility.

The role of the maintenance activities is to have optimum availability of plant and machinery in the conduct of operations, and if an unexpected breakdown occurs, it will be dealt with in the shortest minimum possible time.

Topic Eighteen

REAL ESTATE LAW

How do you get to exercise rights on a property? How do you get to sack tenants and give new tenants a house without the former resisting or refusing your orders?

What makes a property yours even after your demise? There are obviously certain laws and regulations in the society that gives us the power, rights and authority to own properties in line with some due processes.

Real estate law basically explains and educates us on the identification and valuation of a variety of different rights but also the analysis of the many limitations on those rights and the effect the limitations have on value.

The major distinction in real property ownership is the difference between private and public ownership.

Public ownership: This usually takes many forms like streets, roads, utility systems, city halls, and prisons etc, usually owned by Government bodies for the benefit of all citizens.

Most public ownership is created in response to public demand or necessity e.g. when it is necessary to create a parking lot, using the power of eminent domain. These facilities or properties are not usually subject to taxation.

Private ownership: Private ownership real estate can be owned by one or more entities.

Individual ownership is known as "ownership in severalty". However, individuals can hold ownership under certain entities 100% ownership of the stock corporation that owns real estate.

Concurrent ownership includes joint tenancy, tenancy by entirety and tenancy in common. Joint tenancy is ownership by two or more persons with the right of survivorship. Upon death of one person, ownership automatically becomes vested in the other. Tenancy by entirety is an estate held by a husband and wife in which neither has a disposable interest during the lifetime of the other, except by joint action. Tenancy in common is an estate held by two or more persons, with an undivided interest. In this estate, there is no survivorship, which means one tenant may sell an undivided interest without the approval of the other.

SPECIAL FORMS OF OWNERSHIP

(i) **Condominium ownership:** This is a form of ownership of separate units or portions of multi-unit buildings e.g. a 1000 housing unit estate. The owner simply holds title to an individual unit and an undivided partial interest in the common areas of the total condominium project e.g. parking space, outer walls, foundation, recreation areas etc. The unit can be leased, mortgaged or sold.

(ii) **Co-operative ownership:** A stock corporation is organized, acquires title to an apartment building, prices the various apartments and issues an authorized number of shares at a specified value. Individuals then purchase shares of stock with the price per unit equivalent to the shares that must be purchased. Each owner purchases a proprietary lease on a specific apartment and is obligated to make a monthly payment.

(iii) **Timesharing:** This is the sale of either limited ownership interest or rights to use and occupy residential apartments or hotel rooms.

RESTRICTIONS ON OWNERSHIP

Public ownership of real property rights is guaranteed by a country's constitution but subject to certain restrictions known as the four powers of Government, namely taxation, eminent domain, police power and escheat:

(i) **Taxation:** This is the right of the government to raise revenue through assessments of goods, products and rights.

(ii) **Eminent domain:** This is the right of the government to take private property for public use upon payment of just compensation.

(iii) **Police power:** This is the right of the government through which property is regulated to protect public safety, health, morals and general welfare.

(iv) **Escheat:** This is the right that gives government ownership of a property when the owner dies without a will and heirs.

PRIVATE RESTRICTIONS ON OWNERSHIP

Private restrictions on property ownership can limit the use or development of a property and the manner in which ownership can be conveyed, e.g. easement, right of way, party wall.

(i) **Easement:** Is an interest in real property that transfers use but not ownership of a portion of an owners' property.
(ii) **Right of way:** This is the right to pass over the land of another in some particular way or path e.g. for railroads, highway purposes, pole lines etc
(iii) **Party wall:** This is a common wall erected along the boundary adjoining two properties, which the owners have a common right of use.

Topic Nineteen

RESIDENTIAL PROPERTY DEVELOPMENT

The nature of houses to suit different cultures, weather and climates, religious orientations, style and appeal vary from one geographical location to another, one country to another and one continent to another.

For example, a fireplace in Saudi Arabia is obviously out of place, or an air conditioner in Alaska, U.S.A. While some architectural designs are meant to dispel heat in certain regions and continents of the world, other designs are meant to trap the heat, due to different climatic and topographic differences.

Residential Property Development: Trends in polygamous, single family and apartments design change with time, and building components such as balconies, porches, fire places, dining rooms, large kitchens and entry halls may be included or excluded.

Housing standards vary widely for different income levels and regions. A country with a polygamous nature will definitely not appreciate an architectural design that limits space and privacy, like a three bedroom with a single toilet and so on.

To evaluate the functional utility of residential buildings, appraisers should analyze standard market expectations e.g. the functional utility of a residential home should be its layout, accommodation of specific activities, adequacy and ease and cost of maintenance.

In general, more people have better housing today than the past years, because many amenities are now considered necessities and their inclusion is not taken for granted.

FACTORS THAT INFLUENCE REAL PROPERTY VALUES:

The value of real property is reflected and affected by some forces that influence human activity namely: social trends, economic circumstances, Government regulations and control and environmental conditions.

The interaction of these forces influences the value of every parcel of real estate in the market and an understanding of value-influencing forces is fundamental to the appraisal of real property.

Let's take a brief and closer look at these forces:

(i) **Social forces:** This is primarily related to population characteristics, because the demographic composition of the population determines the potential value of real estate. The total population age, gender, rate of family formation and dissolution, education, law and order and lifestyle options.
(ii) **Economic forces:** Factors like employment, economic base of regions and communities, cost and availability of mortgage credit, occupancy rates, rental and price patterns of existing properties, construction costs and new developments all affect values.

(iii) **Government forces:** Political and legal activities can all have great impact on property values.
(iv) **Environmental forces:** Climatic conditions such as snowfalls, earthquakes, temperature and humidity, topography and soil, toxic contaminants.

The environmental forces that affect the value of a property may be understood in relation to the property's location.

Single family residential districts: Home ownership symbolizes economic prosperity and residents of an area often take an active role in maintaining or enhancing the value of their properties. This is usually achieved through formed associations by owners which often enforce conditions, covenants and restrictions such as crime watch groups, recreational parks, clubs etc.

Multifamily residential districts: In large cities, multifamily residential districts usually cover an extensive area. In smaller cities such districts may be dispersed or limited. They have high rise buildings, row houses, Garden apartments, cooperative apartments, access to shopping centers etc. They have similarities with single-family residential districts, but have a higher density.

RESIDENTIAL LAYOUT CONSIDERATIONS:

Poor plans are easily recognizable by those who make up the market.

Standards usually vary with current trends in a region and neighborhood e.g. culture, religion etc. For example, the location of various rooms can affect the privacy and comfort of a house and thus affect the value, like the master bed room being next to the kitchen or the master bedroom being next to the children's room in a polygamous home.

Topic Twenty

Risk Management

Most often, a lot of actions taken have to be analyzed so as to avoid unfavorable reactions or results.

For instance, you want to travel at night with no spare tire in your car, with no adequate money for fuel and hotel accommodation, or you are in a hurry to go downstairs from a three story building and you decide to jump down. Certain actions need analysis before they are taken. The certainties of failure in your journey or coming down safely from the building, we must admit is very high. Consequently, in everything an individual, organization, State or Country will engage in, there has to be some sort of adverse effects analysis, which is in other words referred to as risk(s).

Definition of Risk: A risk is any "uncertainty" which if it occurs will have an effect on achievement of one or more objectives. This generic definition allows us to apply risk management to a broad range of activities in our daily lives and other business endeavors.

Defining Objectives:

As with any other application area, risk management can be applied at different levels. The key lies in how well we are able to specify our objectives both personal and organizational.

At the highest level, we might say that our aim is to be "happy, healthy, wealthy and wise", and we can identify and manage strategic personal risks which might affect these broad goals.

This might require us to address issues such as our personal relationships, diet and exercise regime, investment and pension policies etc. We might even identify more specific objectives such as get married in ten months, finish building my house in two years, buy a car in the next six months, etc. For all these objectives, we can apply the risk management process to help us reach and achieve them.

THREATS AND OPPORTUNITIES

The process is the same as any other application of risk management.

After defining your objectives, the next step is to identify risks, including threats which could hinder us as well as opportunities which could help us e.g. moving to another job, implications of moving the family to the new job location, school fees for the kids etc.

After risk identification, then comes assessment, estimating the probability and impact of each identified risk to prioritize them for further action.

Simple high/medium/low scales can be used for this, enabling the worst threats and best opportunities to be found.

> Risk assessment should be carried out regularly in order to find and respond to new opportunities and threats.

Risk management is not just for work or business alone. It can help us achieve our personal objectives as well.

While taking risk and winning is fun, prudent businessmen take care to minimize the risk, just as in any risky venture you undertake.

A good risk management system is a continuous process of analysis and communication.

Risk Management: The term risk management is applied in a number of diverse disciplines. People in different fields like statistics, medicine, economics, toxicology, engineering construction etc have all been addressing the field of risk management.

Risk management is a discipline for living with the possibility that future events may cause adverse effects.

For a risk to be understandable it must be clearly expressed, such a statement must include a description of the current conditions that may lead to the loss and description of the loss.

Non-continuous risk management is a risk that is identified and dealt with and not looked at again.

Continuous risk management is a risk that is always re-evaluated for decision making in the phase of a project.

Topic Twenty One

STRATEGIC MANAGEMENT

Strategy: Simply ways and means of achieving a goal or target.

Management: Getting things done through others.

Business Policy: is a guide for making administrative decision.

It is an organization's point of view and established manner of doing business and directing managerial action.

Policy: It is an internal administrative law governing executive decisions and actions within an organization.

Just like countries have laws, religions and clubs, policy also plays a similar role in business.

Policies can be formal or informal and are not meant to substitute decisions, but aid them.

Policies rationally developed are however more advantageous than informal ones because they are economically less wasteful to the organization.

The managers initiate, formulate and recommend policies as they affect their departments, which is done and passed through the CEO to the Board for approval.

BUSINESS FUNCTIONAL POLICIES

Several business policy options exist that could be adopted to effectively handle problems and challenges posed by internal and external environment. These are enumerated as follows:

(i) The personnel policy:
This covers overall policies on personnel of an organization: employment policies, training and development, staff welfare etc.

(ii) The production policy:
The essence is to enable maintain leads in quality of products, reduced cost and ensure ready availability and use of cost efficient means of production.

(iii) The marketing policy:
Companies formulate policies to deal with the opportunities and threats that exist in their environment.

(iv) The finance policy:
Areas of raising funds, investing such funds in assets and distributing returns earned to shareholders.

BUSINESS STRATEGY AND STRATEGIC MANAGEMENT:

This is an analytical thinking and commitment of resources to action.

There is no one best way to create strategy nor is there one best form of organization.

The world is full of contradictions and the effective strategist is one who can live with contradictions, learn to appreciate their causes and effects and reconcile them sufficiently for effective action.

There is no single model or theory that can incorporate all factors that influence major business decisions.

Goals and objectives state what is to be achieved and when results are expected, but do not state how.

Programs specify the step-by-step sequence of actions necessary to achieve major objectives.

The essence of strategy is for a firm to achieve a long-term sustainable advantage over its competitors in every business in which it participates.

Strategic management: is concerned with long range direction or organization and consequently provides a framework for operational management.

Corporate Strategy:

This is the sense of direction for the entire organization and so it identifies the business the organization will engage in.

This strategy usually answers the question: what business are we in?

Business strategy: This deals with a single strategic business unit which should have an identifiable and definable product range, market segment and competitor set.

Functional strategy: There will be a set for each strategic business unit. Each will aim at making the best use of the resources available in order to contribute to the business strategy.

BUSINESS AND ITS ENVIRONMENT

As soon as business is established, it creates its own contact with its environment through its customers, employees and suppliers.

The more successful a business, the more contacts it makes, competitors appear, authorities become interested and new products and markets have to be employed.

It soon becomes involved in the "business game" surrounded by other players on a large pitch, all governed by common factors: economics, demography, politics, culture, ecology, technology etc and all affected by and contributing to change.

One method of understanding the relationship between a business and its environment is to consider the various groups both internal and external that can affect and be affected by the accomplishment of its objectives.

Business is affected by two environmental variables: internal and external. Internal variable factors are manageable and controllable such as sources of supply, company's culture, etc, while external variables are uncontrollable such as political / legal, economic, socio-cultural factors and market environment.

CORPORATE SOCIAL RESPONSIBILITY

Should businesses be concerned with social responsibilities beyond its own economic well being?

Do social concerns affect a company's financial well being?

Corporate social responsibility is the obligation towards society assumed by business. It maximizes its positive effects towards society and minimizes its negative effects.

Legal responsibility: Is to obey at the very least, the local, state, federal and relevant international laws.

Ethical responsibility: Obliging to other laws of the society other than written laws.

Voluntary responsibilities: Activities the society find desirable like community projects, charity contributions etc.

Topic Twenty Two

THE MANAGEMENT OF TEAMS

Teams: There is this saying; two heads are better than one. Teams are replacing individuals as the basic building blocks of organizations. Organizations around the globe are discovering that teams potentially make more creative and informed decisions and coordinate work without the need for close supervision.

Teams are groups of two or more people that interact and influence each other, are mutually accountable for achieving common objectives, and perceive themselves as a social entity within an organization.

All teams exist to fulfill some purpose, such as assembling a product, providing a service, or making an important decision.

Team members are held together by their interdependence and need for collaboration to achieve common goals. All teams require some form of communication so members can coordinate and share common objectives. Team members also influence each other, although some members are more influential than others regarding the team's goals and activities.

All teams are groups because they consist of people with a unifying relationship. But not all groups are teams; some groups are just people assembled together, e.g. employees who meet for lunch are rarely called teams because they have no purpose beyond their social interaction.

Team effectiveness: Refers to how the team affects the organization, individual team members, and the team's existence. Most teams exist to serve some purpose relating to the organization or other system in which the group operates.

Team effectiveness considers the satisfaction and well-being of its members; therefore, it makes sense that effectiveness is partly measured by this need fulfillment. Finally, team effectiveness includes the team's viability—its ability to survive. It must be able to maintain the commitment of its members, particularly during the turbulence of the team's development.

TEAM DESIGN AND FEATURES

Putting together a team is rather like creating an organization. There are several elements to consider and the wrong combination will result in a dysfunctional rather than an effective team. Three main structural elements to consider are task characteristics, team size and team composition.

These elements affect team effectiveness directly as well as indirectly through team processes. The skills and diversity of team members affect team cohesiveness, but also have a direct effect on how well the team performs its task. Similarly, the type of work performed by the team (task characteristics) may influence the type of roles that emerge, but it also has a direct effect on the satisfaction and well-being of team members.

Task Characteristics:

Teams are generally more effective when tasks are clear and easy to implement, because team members can learn their roles more quickly. In contrast, teams with ill-defined tasks require more time to agree on the best division of labor and the correct way to accomplish the goal.

Another important task characteristic is task interdependence. This exists when team members must share common inputs to their individual tasks, need to interact in the process of executing their work, or receive outcomes that are partly determined by the performance of others.

Recent evidence indicates that task interdependence creates an additional sense of responsibility among team members which motivates them to work together rather than alone.

Team Size:

The optimal team size depends on several factors, such as the number of people required to complete the work and the amount of coordination needed to work together. The general rule is that teams should be large enough to provide the necessary competencies and perspectives to perform the work, yet small enough to maintain efficient coordination and meaningful involvement of each member. Larger teams are typically less effective because members consume more time and effort coordinating their roles and resolving differences. Individuals have less opportunity to participate and consequently, are less likely to feel that they are contributing to the team's success.

TEAM COMPOSITION:

With respect to motivation, every member must have sufficient drive to perform the task in a team environment. Team members must be motivated to agree on the goal, work together rather than alone and abide by the team's rules of conduct. Employees with a collectivist orientation tend to perform better in work teams, whereas those with a strong individualist orientation tend to perform better alone.

Employees must possess the skills and knowledge necessary to accomplish the team's objectives. Each person needs only to possess some of the necessary skills, but the entire group must have the full set of competencies. Each team member's competencies need to be known to other team members.

TEAM DIVERSITY:

Another important dimension of team composition is the diversity of team members.

Homogeneous teams include members with common technical expertise, ethnicity, experiences or values, whereas heterogeneous teams have members with diverse personal characteristics and backgrounds.

Heterogeneous teams experience more interpersonal conflict and take longer to develop. They are susceptible to "faultiness", i.e. hypothetical dividing lines that may split a team into subgroups along gender, ethnic, professional, or other dimensions that may eventually break the team apart.

In contrast, members of homogeneous teams experience higher satisfaction, less conflict and better interpersonal relations. Consequently, homogeneous teams tend to be more effective on tasks requiring a high degree of cooperation and coordination, such as emergency response teams.

Although heterogeneous teams are more difficult to develop, they are generally more effective than homogeneous teams on complex projects and problems requiring innovative solutions. This is because people from different backgrounds see a problem or opportunity from different perspectives. Heterogeneous team members also solve complex problems more easily because they usually have a broader knowledge base.

A team's diversity may give it more legitimacy or allow its members to obtain a wider network of cooperation and support in the organization

References

Abubakar, S., Dongs, I.S, and Dangana, A.E (2010). **A Practical Approach to Project Management,** Zamani Printing Press, Bauchi, Bauchi-State-Nigeria.

Armstrong, M. (2006). **Human Resource Management Practice**, Tenth Edition, Kogan Page Limited.

Audu, D. E (2005). **The Secrets of Business Success**, Hosanna Printing press Jos, Plateau State-Nigeria.

Appraisal Institute (2001). **The Appraisal of Real Estate**, Twelfth Edition, USA.

Brown, S and Peterson, R.A. "The effect of effort on sales performance and job satisfaction." Journal of Marketing 58 (1994). Pp. 70-80; Behrman, D.N. and Perrault, N.D Jr., "A Role Stress Model of the performance and satisfaction of Industrial salespersons," Journal of Marketing 48 (1984). Pp. 9-21.

Buhler, P. (2002). **Human Resources Management**, Adams Media, F+W Publications, Inc, USA.

Cole, G. (2004). **Management Theory and Practice**, Sixth Edition, Book Power.

Dongs,I.S, Dangana, A. E., Atabo, A.A. (2009). **Modern Theories and Practice of Management,** Zamani Printing Press, Bauchi, Bauchi-State-Nigeria.

Drury, C. (2004). **Management and Cost Accounting**, Sixth Edition, Book power.

Klaas, B. S And Wheeler H.N. "Managerial Decision Making about Employee Discipline: A Policy Capturing Approach, "Personnel Psychology 43 (1990).

Kotler, P. (1997). **Marketing Management, Analysis, Planning, Implementation and Control,** Ninth Edition, Prentice Hall, Harlow-England.

Kotler P., Armstrong, G., Saunders, J. and Wong, V. (2002). **Principles of Marketing**, Third Edition, Prentice Hall, Harlow-England.

Latham,G.P and Huber V.L, "Schedules of Reinforcement: Lessons from the past and issues for the future," Journal of Organizational Behavior Management 13 (1992), pp. 125-49.

Pfeiffer, J. **New Directions for Organization theory: Problems and prospects** (New York: Oxford University Press,).

Probst, G.F.B. "Practical knowledge Management: A Model that Works, "Prism (Second Quarter 1998), pp 17-23; Miles, G., Miles, R,E. Perrone, V. and Edvinsson, L. "Some Conceptual and Research Barriers to the utilization of Knowledge, "California Management Review Barriers to the Utilization of Knowledge, "California Management Review 40 (spring 1998), pp 281-288; Nevis, E.C., Bella, A.J.D and Gould, J.M "Understanding Organizations as learning systems," Sloan Management Review 36 (Winter

1995), pp 78-85; G. Huber, Organizational Learning: The Contributing Processes and Literature." Organizational Science 2 (1991), pp. 88-115.

Tushman, M.L., Nadler, M.B. and Nadler D.A., **Competing by Design: The Power of Organizational Architecture** (New York: Oxford University Press, 1997).

Robock, S.H., Simmonds, K., Zwick, J. (1977). **International Business and Multinational Enterprises, Richard D. Irwin, Inc USA.**

Robbins, S.P. and Judge, T.A. (2007). **Organizational Behavior**, Twelfth Edition, Prentice Hall of India Private Limited.

www.ingramcontent.com/pod-product-compliance
Lightning Source LLC
Chambersburg PA
CBHW030753180526
45163CB00003B/1011